EXERCISES AND PROBLEMS
IN PROFESSIONAL RESPONSIBILITY

SECOND EDITION

EXERCISES AND PROBLEMS
IN PROFESSIONAL RESPONSIBILITY

SECOND EDITION

Robert P. Burns
Thomas F. Geraghty
Steven Lubet

© 1994, 2001
By
THE NATIONAL INSTITUTE FOR TRIAL ADVOCACY, INC.

Reproduction Permission
National Institute for Trial Advocacy
Notre Dame Law School
Notre Dame, Indiana 46556
(800) 225-6482   Fax (219) 271-8375
E-mail: *nita.1@nd.edu*
www.nita.org

Adapted with permission and gratitude from materials from the National Institute for Trial Advocacy by James H. Seckinger

Burns, Robert P., Thomas F. Geraghty, and Steven Lubet, *Exercises and Problems in Professional Responsibility* Second Edition (NITA, 2001).

ISBN 1–55681–644–8

7/01

EXERCISES AND PROBLEMS
IN PROFESSIONAL RESPONSIBILITY

CONTENTS

Exercises

Problems

INTRODUCTION

These materials apply the simulation method to the study of professional responsibility. Each major area of professional responsibility is the subject of an exercise in which students are required to perform important lawyering tasks fully in role. Some student performances will be the subject of formal "disciplinary hearings" in which other students, acting as prosecutors and defense counsel, argue the propriety of the actual decisions that the student lawyers made. Most of the exercises are simply followed by discussion.

The rules and codes of professional responsibility are almost always merely "abridgements" or condensations of an envisioned form of "good practice." Good practice is best learned by practicing, but in an environment that has the heightened ethical self-consciousness that these exercises and material provide. Otherwise the one or other set of rules, such as the Model Rules of Professional Conduct, which we generally follow, can become a ballet of bloodless categories, divorced from the reality that they are intended to control. This makes it harder, we believe, for a young lawyer actually to recognize ethical issues as they arise in the course of his or her practice.

Since every relevant variation in a given fact pattern cannot be plausibly woven into each simulation, the exercises are supplemented by problems that complete the basic picture. A few issues that do not lend themselves to simulation are addressed by problems alone. Faculty members may also perform demonstrations of a number of lawyering tasks that raise further issues. And if there is an emphasis in the materials, it is on those issues that arise in litigation and negotiation.

Several times during the semester each student will be asked to perform important lawyering tasks. These include interviewing witnesses, counseling clients, negotiating settlements, and conducting the direct and cross-examinations of witnesses. These exercises will be fully in role: students will act as attorneys performing each of the tasks. Some students will serve as prosecutors and as defense counsel in "disciplinary hearings". Thus each class member will see and experience the world of professional responsibility from a number of key perspectives within it. Virtually all the exercises and problems are taken from two case files, one criminal (*State v. Mitchell*) and the other civil (*MacIntyre v. Easterfield*). Summaries of those case files follow.

Exercises & Problems in Professional Responsibility

THE JOE MITCHELL MURDER CASE

At 10 P.M. on September 10, YR-2[1], Leslie Thompson was shot dead as she stood on her stepmother's front porch. Her stepmother, Brooke Thompson, told the police when they arrived moments later that she had seen Leslie's estranged husband, Joe Mitchell, drive up to the curb in front of her house and fire one shot through Leslie's heart. Almost immediately, the police drove to Joe Mitchell's rooming house, where they found him. On the floor were his wet clothes and a .38 caliber revolver nearby, the kind of gun used to kill Leslie. Joe seemed shaken by the news of the attack on his wife and agreed to accompany the police to the station. When the police learned that Leslie had been pronounced dead, they arrested Joe for the murder of his wife. The detective who initially investigated the killing believed that Joe was innocent and suspected Brooke Thompson, but his views did not prevail. Joe denied any involvement in the crime.

Leslie's father, Brooke's husband, died when Leslie was fourteen. Brooke then sent Leslie to boarding school for high school and then to secretarial school in New York. After returning to Nita City, Leslie lived with Brooke for a short time while working in a bank. Leslie fell in love with and ultimately married Joe Mitchell, an ex-Marine and unpublished mystery story writer, who supported himself by pumping gas. Brooke was strenuously opposed to the marriage, and in fact, refused to come to the wedding.

Joe's insistence on a writing career and his refusal to work at a conventional job became a source of tension in the marriage. In fewer than two years, Leslie left Joe to return to Brooke's house. There followed frequent angry scenes at Brooke's as Joe tried to convince Leslie to return to him. She and Brooke insisted that Joe get a "real job." Joe accused them of trying to destroy his dream and seemed particularly resentful of Brooke's role in preventing reconciliation. On the night before Leslie was killed, he wrote a bitter letter to Leslie blaming Brooke for destroying their marriage, expressing his "hate" for Brooke, and claiming that he would make Brooke and Leslie "regret" what they had done.

It did appear that Brooke was happy about the imminent end of Leslie's marriage. She had never liked Joe. Also, according to the terms of her husband's will, she would lose control over certain assets after Leslie remained married for four years.

Joe admitted that he was looking for Leslie on the night on September 10, but claimed it was in order to continue to persuade her to return to him. He had just received a letter and a check for $500 as an advance on his first script and, he said, he hoped that this might change things. Earlier in the evening he had shown up at Brooke's house, and then at a movie theater where Leslie had gone alone, and then had gone to a local bar where he had four beers. As he told it, he then picked up a .38 caliber revolver that was being repaired at Ravenna's gun shop. He returned to his rooming house, where he was seen coming in between 9:40 and 9:55 P.M. (It turned out that the ballistics tests were

---

1. The year designations in this book are as follows. YR-0 designates the year in which the exercise is being performed. If the exercise is being performed in 2002, then 2002 is YR-0. YR-1, YR-2, and YR-3 denote respectively years one, two, and three years in the past. Thus if the exercise is performed in 2002, YR-1 is 2001, YR-2 is 2000 and so forth. YR+1, YR+2, YR+3 denote respectively years one, two, and three years into the future. Thus if the exercise is being performed in 2002, YR+1 is 2003 and so on.

inconclusive and that there was no evidence that Joe's gun had been fired, though a quick cleaning might account for that.) Joe was next seen at the rooming house at 10:30 P.M. and prosecution claimed that it was physically possible for Joe to have made the round trip undetected from the rooming house to the Thompson home and back.

Several things gave pause to the investigating detective, Pat Slyviak. The position of the body suggested, though not conclusively, that the bullet had come from inside the house. Brooke Thompson was the beneficiary of a considerable life insurance policy on Leslie. Brooke had once before shot a man in "self-defense" while collecting rents in a run-down apartment building she owned. She admitted owning a .38, but she claimed it had been stolen, and was beyond testing. There was also a rumor on the street about an attempt to arrange a hit by a thug named Jerry Young, on a woman who may have been named Thompson. Soon after Joe was arrested, the police received an enigmatic letter claiming that the anonymous author had skipped town after being paid to kill someone who may have been Leslie. While it was not physically impossible for Joe to have been the killer, the distance between his rooming house and the Thompson residence made it difficult. Further, even if Brooke was not somehow involved in Leslie's death, the conditions under which the killing took place did not allow for a very reliable identification, particularly by someone who bore a deadly hatred for Joe.

On the other hand, there was Joe's obvious motive to try to kill either Leslie or Brooke. His letter of the day before certainly read like a threat. He had admittedly picked up his gun a short time before the killing. He had been drinking and was looking for Leslie. Joe had often bragged that he was an expert marksman. And perhaps significantly, a second letter had arrived from the studio telling him that the advance had been a mistake and that they could make no commitment to produce his story. The final straw? But had he even seen the retraction letter? It was unclear.

Exercises & Problems in Professional Responsibility

THE JESSE MACINTYRE SLANDER CASE

On July 17, YR-2, Jesse MacIntyre stormed out of Ross Easterfield's mansion, where she worked as a live-in maid, and went to live at an institution for women maintained by the St. James Episcopal Church. Jesse told her friend, the Reverend Taylor, that Easterfield had, within the hearing of another maid, accused her of stealing a piece of his wife's jewelry. She could not work where she was so mistreated.

Almost immediately, Jesse began to look for employment. She came to believe that wherever she turned, her path was blocked by Ross Easterfield's malicious slanders. In particular, she was denied a job which she felt sure was hers at the Nita City Athletic Club, on whose board Easterfield happened to sit. And she was denied the services of an Employment Agency following a conversation between Ross and the agency manager. She could find work nowhere else. Finally, she was driven to filing a lawsuit against Easterfield for the slander that she believed was preventing her from earning a living. She felt justified in doing this especially when the missing piece of jewelry turned up several weeks later in the Easterfield library, albeit near a book whose author's name was "MacIntyre."

This was not Jesse's first involvement with the legal process. After leaving the orphanage where she grew up, she met one Frank Holman, whom she dated several times. She was unaware of his criminal record and also didn't know that he would try an armed robbery of a convenience store while she waited outside in a car. She was arrested and charged as an accomplice and intimidated by her incompetent lawyer into accepting a plea bargain and a short term in the penitentiary. Reverend Taylor was her chaplain and, upon her release, arranged for the job in the Easterfield home.

Ross Easterfield was a wealthy man who owned a real estate business. There is no doubt that his wife, Kerry Easterfield, did have a habit of misplacing her jewelry around the house and blaming other people. Though he claimed that he was interested to know on July 17 where the missing piece of jewelry was, and wanted Jesse to help him find it, he denied that he accused Jesse of anything on that date. He admitted that he found her refusal to help them strange and her outburst somewhat suspicious. He admitted speaking with agents of the club and the employment agency, but denied accusing Jesse of theft to either of them. There was, however, evidence that Easterfield had sought to pressure a financial institution to whom Jesse had made an application for a loan to file criminal charges against her for possibly innocent misstatements on a loan application. This latter, the plaintiff argued, was evidence of true malice, the existence of which would defeat Easterfield's qualified immunity for statements made to the athletic club's director and to the employment agency.

There were serious disputes about what it was that Easterfield actually said on the morning of July 17. Also in dispute were Ross's statements to Lee Marlow (the executive director of the athletic club) and to Reeve Winsor (the official from the Employment Agency). Ross generally denied ever directly accusing Jesse of stealing. In his account he was simply conducting an innocent inquiry in his home and was just trying to tell the truth to prospective employers who had a right to know what he could tell them. (Ross also argued that nothing he said could actually have been the proximate cause of Jesse's rejection at the club, since the club had a policy of never hiring ex-convicts. The actual existence of such a policy was strongly disputed.) Easterfield also claimed that he could not reasonably have known that the other maid, Kelly Emerson, was right outside the library door and could hear

Exercises & Problems in Professional Responsibility

some of what went on inside. And it is at least possible that Ross could claim that Jesse did in fact try to steal the brooch, a plan that was frustrated by Ross's inquiries, forcing her to leave the brooch "hidden" behind the "MacIntyre" book in the library. (Truth would be a complete defense to a claim of slander.)

Jesse gave a different account of what was said in the library on July 17, one where it was apparent that Easterfield was accusing her. She also maintained that Marlow's account of what Easterfield said at the club was the product of bias in favor of one of the directors, one with a reputation for being vindictive. The circumstantial evidence, Jesse argued, strongly suggested that she would have gotten the job without Ross's gratuitous (and malicious) interference, including a direct accusation of theft. Jesse also maintained that the best interpretation of the notes that Winsor took of the conversation with Easterfield strongly suggest a direct accusation of criminal activity.

The case involves specific disputed questions of fact such as, "What exactly was said at a particular time and place?" and "Did Jesse attempt to steal the brooch?" It also involves much broader issues of reasonableness under given circumstances and of state of mind. On these latter questions, the case contains an enormous amount of circumstantial evidence from which different, indeed conflicting, inferences can be drawn.

EXERCISE 1
CLIENT COUNSELING

representing Easterfield

In this exercise students will interview Ross Easterfield on behalf of the law firm. Another student will serve as a senior partner with whom the interviewers may consult after the interview. Easterfield is an important client for whom your firm has done at least a quarter of a million dollars' worth of work in each of the past three years. Ross wants to discuss "increasing the amount and forms of work that your firm is doing for me." The partner in charge of the real estate division has told you that Easterfield's business ventures are an important new source of business and told you, "I want us to accommodate him if we can."

You are to discuss the various sorts of work that Easterfield wants you to do. Conduct any counseling of Mr. Easterfield that you and your colleague deem appropriate. Tell him what you are willing to do and what you cannot do. If there is something that you cannot do, tell him why. If you cannot be sure of what you will do, tell him that. After the interview, confer with your senior partner if necessary. Decide what you will do and communicate your decisions to Easterfield at a second interview.

Your decisions will be evaluated by a student prosecutor for the disciplinary committee, who will present any case against you to the committee. Defense counsel will defend your decisions. Another student will be assigned to play the part of the managing partner of your firm who will have a strong, though not exclusive interest in expansion of the firm's business. The remaining students will play the part of the disciplinary committee, which will determine whether any disciplinary violation has occurred.

In order to advise Ross Easterfield properly, you need to know the following:

(1) The discovery rules that apply in civil cases will require the production of all nonprivileged documents that are reasonably calculated to lead to the discovery of relevant evidence.

(2) Arson is a criminal offense in Nita City, a felony carrying a penalty of up to ten years in prison. If someone dies in an intentionally set fire, the arsonist may be guilty of second degree murder, a felony carrying a maximum penalty of life in prison.

(3) The Federal Bureau of Investigation will investigate those fires which they believe may have been set as part of a scheme to defraud an insurance company that does business in more than one state. As a practical matter, they never investigate a fire where the insurance claim is for less than one million dollars. Arson committed as part of such a scheme is a federal crime and carries a penalty of up to fifteen years in prison.

(4) The Nita "accountability" statute provides for vicarious liability for criminal acts. It provides in relevant part:

A person is legally accountable for the conduct of another when:

Either before or during the commission of an offense, and with the intent to promote or facilitate such commission, he solicits, aids, abets, agrees or attempts to aid, such other person in the planning or commission of the offense. However, a person is not so accountable, unless the statute defining the offense provides otherwise, if:

Before the commission of the offense, he terminates his efforts to promote or facilitate such commission, and does one of the following: wholly deprives his prior efforts of effectiveness in such commission, or gives timely warning to the proper law enforcement authorities, or otherwise makes proper effort to prevent the commission of the offense.

An "accountable" defendant is subject to the same penalties as is the person for whose action the accountable defendant is vicariously liable.

(5) The applicable Open Housing Ordinance provides: "No owner of rental property shall take action with regard to that property with the specific intent to deny a person or persons occupancy of such property because of race, sex, religion, or national origin. Such specific intent may be proven by circumstantial evidence."

The ordinance provides for damages and injunctive relief, but no criminal penalties. *not criminal or fraudulent*

(6) The Nita Retaliatory Eviction Statute provides:

It shall be a defense to an action brought in forcible detainer that such action was brought because the tenant has complained to the local building department about violations of the building code. The tenant shall bear the burden of proof.

The landlord may choose not to renew a lease at the end of its term for any reason, however bad, so long as it is not because the tenant belongs to a protected class under the Open Housing Ordinance or because it is in retaliation for complaints to the building department. However, it is no defense to an eviction that the tenant has complained often to the *landlord* or to others, for example, to tenants' groups.

It is a complete defense for the landlord that he was not aware of complaints to the building department. You know that only one tenant in a thousand will be interested and lucky enough to find a lawyer who will properly assert the defense. And you can always settle with such a person.

The building code itself is a municipal ordinance with which a special court called "Building Court" may order compliance, subject ultimately to criminal contempt penalties. The latter rarely occurs and then only for the worst and most dangerous conditions. In cases that manifest conditions dangerous to "health, safety, and well-being" a court may condemn a building, something courts are reluctant to do given the shortage of low-rent housing.

(7) The Nita Criminal Housing Management Statute provides:

    (a) A person commits the offense of criminal housing management when, having personal management or control of residential real estate, whether as a legal or equitable owner or as a managing agent or otherwise, he recklessly permits the physical condition or facilities of the residential real estate to become or remain in any condition which endangers the health or safety of any person.

    (b) Sentence. Criminal housing management is a Class A misdemeanor. A subsequent conviction for a violation of subsection (a) is a Class 4 felony.

    [A Class A misdemeanor carries a minimum sentence of probation and a maximum of one year in jail and a $20,000 fine. A Class 4 felony carries a minimum sentence of probation and a maximum sentence of three years in the state penitentiary and a $50,000 fine.]

You know that criminal housing management is rarely prosecuted. Since the passage of the statute eight years ago, only three persons have been convicted, and only one served time (thirty days). In all three cases, tenants had been seriously injured because of building defects and there had been extensive press coverage.

* * * * * * *

ASSIGNMENTS:

    (A) Interview Ross Easterfield. Inform him of what you are willing to do for him and what you are not. If, in a particular case, you are uncertain of what you are willing to do, consult with the senior partner. After consulting, inform Easterfield of what you will do and why. Conduct any counseling of Mr. Easterfield you deem appropriate.

    (B) Serve as a senior partner in the firm. Consult with the associates who interviewed Easterfield and decide what the firm will do.

    (C) Identify any violations of the Model Rules of Professional Conduct you believe the lawyers committed. Your teacher may ask you to make a formal presentation before a disciplinary committee of your classmates.

(D) Defend the interviewers for any alleged violation of the Model Rules.

(E) Defend the partner for any alleged violation of the Model Rules.

(F) Serve as the managing partner, whose interest is to expand the firm's business without violating any ethical rules.

(G) Serve as the disciplinary committee. Hear the arguments of counsel and render a decision on any issues presented. If there has been a violation, determine an appropriate penalty.

EXERCISE 2
LOYALTY AND ITS LIMITS

Students will interview Brooke Thompson in this class. The interviewers are lawyers in a small Nita firm. You were friends of her husband, the late Judge Thompson, and have known Brooke for some time. You don't like her much, but have a certain loyalty to her stemming from friendship with the late judge.

In order to do the interview and counseling session, you should know the following about the applicable law and practice:

1. You know that the state will always agree to a natural life sentence for murder on a plea of guilty. The prosecution will seek the death penalty if the defendant pleads not guilty and forces a trial. The state has announced that it is seeking the death penalty in Mitchell's case.

2. Two countries with whom the United States does not have extradition treaties are Paraguay and Chile. However, Chile has voluntarily extradited to the United States the last four persons sought by American authorities.

3. Nita has a criminal statute that proscribes "leaving the jurisdiction with the specific intent to avoid prosecution on a criminal charge, whether or not formal proceedings have actually begun."

4. Nita law prohibits the payment of life insurance proceeds to a person who "performed the act which caused the death of the covered individual, with the intention that the person die or suffer great bodily harm, or with the knowledge that death would very probably be the result of his action." The life insurance policy on Leslie contains language that tracks the statute. If the insurance company believed that Brooke was the killer, it would file a declaratory judgment action to be relieved of any obligation under the policy.

5. You believe that a criminal defense lawyer conducting an interview of a prosecution witness will have little regard for ferreting out the real truth of the matter. Instead the lawyer, who will be accompanied by a person who can take the stand to impeach the witness if she deviates from her statement (a so-called "prover"), will seek to gain admissions that will weaken the trial testimony. And merely telling the story an additional time will almost inevitably generate inconsistencies that will damage the effectiveness of the witness. Still, you believe that the trial is more likely to arrive at the truth when both sides have an opportunity to interview adverse witnesses before trial and avoid surprise. You are especially convinced of this in criminal cases where the police have had a full opportunity to "interview" the defendant under unfavorable conditions at the station house.

6. As in most states, in criminal cases there are no depositions or other forms of compulsory pretrial interviews in Nita. Witnesses are free to speak to lawyers or not before trial.

7. The Nita "accountability" statute provides in relevant part:

A person is legally accountable for the conduct of another when:

Either before or during the commission of an offense, and with the intent to promote or facilitate such commission, he solicits, aids, abets, agrees, or attempts to aid such other person in the planning or commission of the offense. However, a person is not so accountable, unless the statute defining the offense provides otherwise, if:

Before the commission of the offense, he terminates his efforts to promote or facilitate such commission, and does one of the following: wholly deprives his prior efforts of effectiveness in such commission, gives timely warning to the proper law enforcement authorities, or otherwise makes proper effort to prevent the commission of the offense.

ASSIGNMENTS:

(A) Interview and counsel Brooke Thompson.

(B) Identify any violations of the Model Rules of Professional Conduct you believe the lawyers committed. Be prepared to justify your views.

(C) Defend the interviewers and counselors for any alleged violations of the rules.

(D) Serve as the disciplinary committee. Hear the arguments of counsel and render a decision on any issues presented. If there has been a violation, determine an appropriate penalty.

EXERCISE 3
DUTIES TO CLIENT AND COURT IN THE PRESENTATION OF TESTIMONY

In this problem, one student will prepare Jesse MacIntyre to testify *only* on what occurred in the library on July 17. Your review of Jesse's deposition gives you some concern that her belief that Ross accused her in the library may not be well-founded. Especially unhelpful is Jesse's admission that it was mainly Ross's actions and facial expressions (which Kelly Emerson could not see) that convinced Jesse that he was accusing her. You are especially concerned that an unfounded belief on Jesse's part in Ross's culpability for the library incident might lead the jury to conclude that Jesse is oversensitive and unworthy of any compensation for the other slanders. You are hoping to obtain more concrete testimony from Jesse that shows that Easterfield really did accuse her.

After preparing Jesse to testify, you will then present Jesse's direct testimony concerning *only* what occurred in the library, and then take any steps necessary in the course of that examination. The Court will be very indulgent in allowing you any recesses you may need in the course of Jesse's testimony.

Before you interview Jesse, you should carefully review her deposition account of what occurred that day. The transcript is attached.

* * * * * *

ASSIGNMENTS:

(A) Prepare Jesse to testify about what occurred in the library on July 17.

(B) Conduct Jesse's direct examination about July 17.

(C) Identify any violations of the Model Rules you believe the lawyers committed. Be prepared to justify your views.

(D) Defend the attorney for any alleged violations.

(E) Serve as the disciplinary committee. Hear the arguments of counsel and render a decision on any issues presented. If there has been a violation, determine an appropriate penalty.

Exercises & Problems in Professional Responsibility

EXCERPT FROM JESSE MACINTYRE'S DEPOSITION

I had seen Mrs. Easterfield wearing it the night before at around 8 P.M., when they left for the concert at the club. It was beautiful and I had always admired it. I heard from the other housekeeper that it was worth $25,000 to $35,000. But Mrs. Easterfield was terribly careless about her jewelry and she was constantly misplacing it and then forgetting where she had put it. She was careless about money too. I was always picking it up and hiding it for her so that some deliveryman would not walk off with it. I told her that if she couldn't find some money she should look for it in the video cassette case for "Jesse James Rides Again." That's where I always put it.

I went upstairs and looked for the brooch, but I did not see it anywhere on her dresser. It was about 9:30 A.M. when I went upstairs, and I had planned to go to St. James Church for services at 10:30 A.M., so I only looked for the brooch for about four or five minutes. I came back downstairs and told Mrs. Easterfield that I couldn't find her brooch on the dresser, and that I had to get ready for church. I said to her, "You know it will turn up. It always does." Mrs. Easterfield didn't say anything, and so I left and went upstairs.

I went to my room to get ready for church. I was in my room for about twenty to twenty-five minutes. I came downstairs around 10:15 A.M. to go to church. I was going to the front door to leave when I heard Mr. Easterfield call me from the library. I went into the library and both Mr. and Mrs. Easterfield were there. He was standing next to his desk and he told me to sit down. I told him that it was my Sunday off and I was in a hurry to get to church. I wasn't angry, I was just in a hurry so I wouldn't be late for church.

I told him that I had to catch a bus or I would miss church. He said he knew that, but this wouldn't take long if I told the truth. His emphasis on the word "truth" and angry tone of voice concerned me and made me feel uncomfortable. Also he called me "Miss," which was unusual, as he always called me "Jesse" or "Miss MacIntyre." I became nervous and felt uncomfortable. I didn't have any idea what he was talking about—what he wanted to know the "truth" about. I said to Mr. Easterfield something like, "What's going on here? You're making me feel very uncomfortable."

Mr. Easterfield then asked me if I had seen his wife's diamond brooch at any time that morning. I told him that I had looked for

Exercises & Problems in Professional Responsibility

it, but I couldn't find it on Mrs. Easterfield's dresser, where she had asked me to look for it. Then he said in a still angrier tone of voice, "What took you so long, why were you gone so long just to look on my wife's dresser?"

I started to tell him that I was gone for only a few minutes before I came back downstairs to tell Mrs. Easterfield that the brooch wasn't on her dresser, but before I could say anything he said: "Now Miss, tell us the truth, what did you do with the brooch—where did you hide it?" When he said that, he was walking toward me, and he came to within two or three feet of me, for a split second I thought he was going to hit me. I had seen him jump up and shake a temporary housekeeper who had spilled coffee on him at breakfast. He's a big man and he really shook her hard. I was afraid.

From his words and appearance, I felt that he was accusing me of stealing the brooch. I couldn't believe what was happening and I was terribly hurt. During the time in the library Mrs. Easterfield continually pursed her lips and turned her head away "in disgust" whenever I tried to say anything. I told him that he had no right to accuse me of stealing the brooch, that it was probably just misplaced like her jewelry usually is, and he knew better than to accuse me of being a thief. His accusations hurt me deeply. I burst into tears and ran out of the room. I went to my room and packed my bags. I just couldn't stay there under those circumstances.

[At this point in her deposition, the following questions were asked and answers given:

Q.   Why do you claim that he was accusing you of theft?

A.   Well, it was clear to me that he was.

Q.   Why?

A.   Well, his threatening actions mainly. And the expression on his face when he talked. What he said, too.

Q.   But your conclusion, let us call it, that he was accusing you came mainly from his actions and his facial expressions, right?

A.   Mainly.

Q.   I'm showing you now what we'll mark as Deposition Exhibit Number 7 and ask you if you recognize this as the Complaint that you filed in this case?

A.   Yes, that's the complaint.

Q.   Did you read the complaint before it was filed?

A.   Yes.

Q.   And were the statements in it true-to-fact and accurate when you read it?

A.   Yes.

Q.   You didn't tell your lawyer to change it, did you?

A.   No.

Q.   And it said that "On Sunday, July 17, Mr. Easterfield said within the hearing of Kelly Emerson, 'Miss MacIntyre has stolen a diamond brooch.' "

A.   Yes, that's right.

Q.   Now, did you ever hear Mr. Easterfield say, "Miss MacIntyre had stolen a diamond brooch"?

A.   Well, no, I didn't.

Q.   But you didn't tell your lawyers that, did you?

A.   What do you mean?

Q.   You did not say to them, "Don't put that in there because it isn't true," did you?

A.   Well, no. I thought they knew what they needed to put in there.

Q.   In order to win this case.

A.   I suppose.

Q.   And you just said, "Whether it's true or not, just put it in if it will help me get some money from Ross Easterfield."

MR. JANUS.   Objection. I think we're getting a little argumentative now.

Q.   You also say in the complaint that Mr. Easterfield did various things "with malice."

A.   Yes.

Q.   Now, in the two years you worked at the Easterfields, did Ross Easterfield once act maliciously towards you?

MR. JANUS.   Objection, calls for a legal conclusion.

Q.   I'm not asking it in the legal sense. You may answer the question.

A.   No. Not maliciously.]

Exercise 3—Duties to Client and Court in the Presentation of Testimony

I finished packing, and when I came downstairs to leave, Mr. and Mrs. Easterfield were in the hall near the front door. I told them that if they thought I was a thief, I just couldn't stay there any longer. I said, "After all this time, now you're calling me a thief." They said nothing. I was walking toward the front door as I said that.

I picked up my bag and went to the front door to leave. When I tried to open the door with my heavy bag, Mr. Easterfield didn't even offer to open the door for me. I had to put my bag down and open the door myself. When I got the door open, Mr. Easterfield reached for the bag, but I picked it up and walked out.

EXERCISE 4
DISTRIBUTION OF AUTHORITY BETWEEN CLIENT AND LAWYER

In this exercise, students will interview a potential witness who has been identified by the client. After interviewing the potential witness, you will discuss with a partner at your firm the question of whether or not to call the witness. You will then discuss the question with Joe Mitchell and make a decision which you will announce and explain to the class.

Joe Mitchell has told you about "an old Marine buddy" who may be able to "help us out." The man's name is Daniel Kiley. Joe says that Kiley claims to have seen something interesting that may be useful for the case. He says that this is all he knows and says that you should talk to Kiley.

It is just before trial and you must both find out what Kiley has to say and decide whether to put him on the stand. Some time ago you discussed with Joe an enigmatic letter which the police received soon after Joe's arrest. In your discussion, Joe said that he had not heard of the letter before your conversation with him. The letter is attached.

In order to deliberate effectively, you need to know several things about the law of impeachment (discrediting) of witnesses. A witness may be impeached on his cross-examination through an inquiry into his bias in favor of the party on whose behalf he is testifying. This usually means that the cross-examiner may reveal to the jury past events or relationships that may serve to show special loyalty to a party. Further, a witness may usually be impeached by the presentation of evidence that the witness has been convicted of any felony or any crime involving dishonesty or false statement. (There are refinements of these doctrines but they will not be significant here.)

It is also helpful to know that out-of-court statements by persons who are not available to testify at trial, are usually admissible if those statements would tend to expose the declarant to criminal liability. (The name for such a statement is "declaration against penal interest.") Such statements may also be used to provide the authentication for an exhibit, such as the attached letter. (Again, the limitations on this doctrine are not significant here.)

* * * * * * *

ASSIGNMENTS:

(A) Interview Kiley. After the interview with Kiley, discuss with a partner at your firm the issues that the interview raises. After consulting with the partner, counsel Joe Mitchell about whether or not you will call Kiley. After your discussion with Joe, explain to the class why you will or will not call Kiley as a witness.

(B) As a partner, consult with the associate who interviewed Kiley.

(C) Identify any violations of the Model Rules you believe the lawyers committed. Be prepared to justify your views.

(D) Defend the interviewer(s) for any alleged violations of the Rules.

(E) Serve as the disciplinary committee. Hear the arguments of counsel and render a decision on any issues presented. If there has been a violation, determine an appropriate penalty.

Dear Police:

You don't know who I am and I'd like to keep it that way. The old witch paid me to knock off her little precious. I took the money and ran. I guess she made other plans—quite resourceful. I've got my dollars and I'm feeling a little sorry for the stiff she's stuck it to. She never knew my name and so I think I can afford this little noble gesture. I'm out of your sick little city. Use your heads for a change.

With all "DUE" respect,

    A man who is telling the truth

Exercises & Problems in Professional Responsibility

EXERCISE 5
INVESTIGATION, DISCOVERY, AND CONTACTS WITH WITNESSES

You represent Jesse MacIntyre. You receive a telephone call from Lee Marlow. About a year has passed since she gave her deposition. [A summary of her deposition is attached.] You expect to go to trial in a year or so. Marlow tells you that she wants to come to your office to have a chat. You have invited her to come in this afternoon. You know that after Marlow gave the account of her conversation with Easterfield at the club that is recounted in the attached summary, you asked the following question, and Marlow gave the following answer:

Q. Other than what you have said, did Mr. Easterfield say anything more to you during the conversation at the club on July 23?

A. No.

* * * * * * * *

ASSIGNMENTS:

(A) Discuss the upcoming conversation with Marlow with your partner. Determine who should be present and how you should proceed. Interview Marlow.

(B) Prosecute the interviewer(s) for any violations of the Rules.

(C) Defend the interviewers for any alleged violations of the Rules.

(D) Serve as the disciplinary committee. Hear the arguments of counsel and render a decision on any issues presented. If there has been a violation, determine an appropriate penalty.

Exercises & Problems in Professional Responsibility

LEE MARLOW'S DEPOSITION

LEE MARLOW, called to testify on Deposition by Plaintiff and having been duly sworn, testified as follows:

My name is Lee Marlow. I am general manager of the Nita City Athletic Club, 500 Main Street, Nita City, Nita. I was hired by the board of directors and have held this position since YR-5. The club is a private social club with approximately 600 members. We have a large building with a gymnasium, swimming pool, auditorium, restaurant, and rooms for members and their guests. I am in charge of hiring all employees.

In July, YR-2, I placed several advertisements for a hatcheck/coatroom attendant. The ad we placed in the Nita City Tribune is below at page 123. I told my secretary to place the ad, but didn't give her the exact words to include. The second-to-last sentence in it is not really accurate and I didn't tell her to include it. The person we had, resigned. The hatcheck/coatroom is on the first floor in the lobby, and is used for members and guests to check their coats and other articles. We rent the auditorium, 3,500 seats, for concerts, plays, and other activities.

When Miss MacIntyre applied for the job, we had already received four applications and I was considering them. On Friday, July 22, Miss MacIntyre came to the club and I talked to her. She didn't make a written application and I did not require one. We discussed the job. I told her it would pay $125 a week plus tips averaging around $50 to $75 a week, and that it would also include meals at the club. I used the latter figure because I had inquired of the other people employed there in the context of their salary reviews. I wanted to know how much they made from tips in order to determine their base salary. The hours would be from 4 P.M. to 1 A.M., with Thursdays and Sundays off.

Yes, I was impressed with Miss MacIntyre when she applied for the job at the club. Her appearance and manners impressed me quite favorably and she appeared to be just what we wanted. Yes, I must admit that after the initial interview with her, she definitely was the front-runner for the job and I would have hired her if I hadn't received further information about her. I may have called her later that day to get some basic information necessary to have her enrolled as an employee.

Exercises & Problems in Professional Responsibility

No, I didn't hire her right on the spot because there were other applications to review, and also, it's our standard practice to do a thorough background check before we hire any employee. I told Miss MacIntyre that and explained to her that a lot would depend on her character references because we could not hire anyone who was not absolutely honest and trustworthy. I told her that guests often leave valuables in their coats or specifically check items for safekeeping in the cloakroom, and that it was imperative that the club maintain an outstanding reputation for security and safekeeping in the cloakroom.

Miss MacIntyre told me that she was living at the St. James Home for Women, and that she knew Reverend MacKenzie Taylor. I belong to St. James Parish, and I've known Reverend Taylor for some time and have admired his work. He counsels young people and helps them get employment. I have contributed money to his work, and yes, I guess I did tell Miss MacIntyre that I had done so.

When Miss MacIntyre mentioned Reverend Taylor, I told her that if she knew Reverend Taylor, there wasn't much for her to worry about. No, I didn't ask her for any other references or anything about her previous employment. I certainly didn't suspect that she had difficulties with the law and so, of course, I didn't ask her anything about having a criminal record. Yes, she gave the address at the St. James Home, but that alone didn't necessarily suggest to me that she was an ex-convict. I knew that Reverend Taylor works with parolees from prison, but he also does a lot of work with other young women who don't have criminal records. It's my understanding that the St. James Home is not exclusively for parolees from prison. I do contribute to the Weston Foundation, a not-for-profit corporation that works with ex-offenders and has a special emphasis in placing ex-offenders in jobs. I am aware of the evidence cited in their literature that shows recidivism has a strong negative correlation with employment upon release. That's just good common sense.

I didn't ask Miss MacIntyre for other references or anything about her prior employment, as I suppose I was satisfied with Reverend Taylor's name and I knew he would give me a full, complete, and accurate rundown on her character and background. The afternoon that Miss MacIntyre applied, I phoned him, but I couldn't reach him. I then made a mental note to talk to him after church services that Sunday.

As it turned out, however, I never did speak to him about Miss MacIntyre. The next day, Saturday, July 23, YR-2, Mr. Ross Easterfield came into the club to have lunch, and when I saw him, I joined him. I have known him and his wife for several years, and he is a member of our board of directors. Also, at one time he served as president of the club, and he has always been very active in the club. He owns the Easterfield Realty Company and is one of the wealthiest men in the city. He lives at 221 Rolling Hills Lane, Nita City, a very exclusive part of town.

During lunch, Mr. Easterfield and I had a rather general conversation about sports, politics, and how things were going at the club. I happened to mention that I was hiring a new hatcheck/coatroom attendant and that the advertisements we'd placed had produced some excellent applicants. When I mentioned hiring the hatcheck attendant, Mr. Easterfield warned me to be careful in my selection and reminded me of the trouble we had with an employee a few years ago. When Easterfield was president of the club, a cashier stole approximately $1,000 from club funds and we never caught her or got the money back.

I told Mr. Easterfield that I had interviewed four or five of the applicants, it looked like I'd found the right person for the job, she appeared to be the perfect person for the position, and if her character references were satisfactory, I was going to hire her. He asked me to tell him a little bit about her, and so I told him that she was living at the St. James Home and had given Reverend Taylor as a reference. He remarked that it was quite a coincidence, because a girl from the St. James Home, whom Reverend Taylor had sponsored, had worked for him as a housekeeper until she quit last Sunday. He asked me the girl's name and when I told him Jesse MacIntyre, he looked surprised and was momentarily taken aback.

Mr. Easterfield said that this was the same girl who had worked for them as a housekeeper until she quit last Sunday, and that he had originally hired her on the recommendation and urging of Reverend Taylor. He said that she had served time in the state prison for attempted armed robbery of a gas station and had been paroled to Reverend Taylor. Mr. Easterfield said that he knew of her past criminal record before hiring her, but, at Reverend Taylor's urging, he decided to help her and give her a chance to start over. He also mentioned that when Miss MacIntyre was hired, they didn't really need another housekeeper, but Reverend Taylor had been so convincing that he was just too softhearted to refuse.

Then, Mr. Easterfield told me about the circumstances under which Miss MacIntyre had quit her job at the Easterfields' that past Sunday. Mrs. Easterfield had worn her very expensive diamond brooch to the club the night before, and on Sunday morning it was missing. Mr. Easterfield said that he had simply asked Miss MacIntyre if she had seen it or knew anything about where the brooch could be, when suddenly she got all upset, stormed out of the room, packed her bags, and walked out, quitting her job with the Easterfields. He said that she had acted very suspiciously and he wouldn't be surprised if she had taken the brooch.

I asked Mr. Easterfield if he had reported this to the police, and he said "no." He said that from the way she acted, and all the surrounding circumstances, there was probably enough to have her arrested, but that he knew a little about the law of false arrest and he didn't want to get into any trouble, get into a messy situation.

Mr. Easterfield also remarked about how Miss MacIntyre's conduct during the previous week had aroused his suspicions. He said his wife had overheard the girl in a phone conversation with some person, and that she was being threatened if she did not come across with $500. He said his wife heard her say she'd get the money, even if she had to steal for it. He also mentioned that Miss MacIntyre had tried to borrow $500 from him and that he had turned her down.

I told Mr. Easterfield that his comments put a whole new light on things. I remember he said something to the effect that, since he was a member of the board of directors, he had a duty to speak out on all matters connected with the club's affairs.

Because of what he had told me on Saturday, I made no further attempt to reach Reverend Taylor or Miss MacIntyre. I hired another applicant that Monday afternoon, a Miss Martha Van Kirk, who is now working for us, so the job was filled right after I talked to Easterfield.

The next day, Tuesday, July 26, YR-2, Jesse MacIntyre called me and inquired about the job. I told her that the job had been filled and there were no other jobs available at the club at the present time. Later that same day, MacIntyre came to see me at the club. She asked me if I had spoken to Reverend Taylor and I told her that I hadn't. I explained to her that before I had a chance to talk to Reverend Taylor, some other circumstances had come up and the job was filled by another person. She pressed me quite hard on what had happened and why she hadn't gotten the job, but I had to tell her that the information was confidential club business and I couldn't reveal it to her.

I asked her if she had a criminal record and she flared up and asked me how I had found out about it. I told her that it was a matter of public record. She admitted that she had been convicted of a crime and said something to the effect that, if I had contacted Reverend Taylor, he would have explained what had happened.

Jesse MacIntyre was obviously annoyed and almost angry at me. She started talking about Mr. Easterfield and the club and was quite upset. She said that if Mr. Easterfield had accused her of stealing his wife's jewelry, it was a lie, and that both Mr. Easterfield and I had made a terrible mistake. She said something to the effect that Mrs. Easterfield is always misplacing her jewelry and accusing the employees of stealing it, but that it turns up where she had left it. MacIntyre got very upset at Mr. Easterfield and stated that he should have thought of his wife's carelessness before accusing others of stealing. She started to cry and ran out of the club.

I have never been in the Easterfields' home. I know nothing about Mrs. Easterfield having a habit of misplacing her jewelry and then accusing an employee of stealing it. Mr. Easterfield has never mentioned anything about that to me. The first and only time I ever heard anything about it was when Miss MacIntyre mentioned it the day we talked in the club.

Yes, I hired Martha Van Kirk for the position. I had no idea at that time that she had a criminal record, if indeed she had one. No, I didn't ask her. Usually, you can assume that people don't have records.

Well, yes, there were some rumors surrounding the Easterfields at the club. I had heard that the Easterfields had serious marital problems from time to time, including last year. Yes, yes, there was the rumor that Mrs. Easterfield would have divorced Mr. Easterfield long ago, if it weren't for her fear of adjusting to a lower standard of living. There was a rumor that Mrs. Easterfield had become involved with George Williams, one of the tennis instructors at the club, and that he was demanding some money to get out of her life and not to tell Mr. Easterfield. The word was that she was trying to sell some of her jewelry in order to pay him. I confronted him about this relationship with the wife of one of our most prominent members and he told me to mind my own business. He threatened to be "a good deal less discreet" if I pushed it and so I backed off. Well, that gentleman died in a canoeing accident on August 1 of last YR-2. Mrs. Easterfield's mood did seem to improve just after that, I must say.

Around August 3rd or 4th, I received a phone call from Mr. Easterfield, and he told me that the missing diamond brooch had been found. He explained that it had been found by their other housekeeper, Ms. Kelly Emerson, in the library behind a book, and oddly enough, a book with an author named MacIntyre.

When Miss MacIntyre applied for the job at the club, she didn't say anything about having a prior criminal record. Also, she didn't tell me the name of her former employer or anything about the missing brooch and the circumstances of her leaving her job with the Easterfields.

It has been a long-standing policy of the club not to hire anyone who has a prior criminal record or any involvement or difficulty with the law in any respect at all. It is absolutely necessary that the club maintain its outstanding reputation, and our members and guests feel comfortable in the club and be able to fully and completely trust the employees. It's a private club, not a commercial establishment, and we have high standards to live up to. I am sure that I would not have hired Jesse had I known about the criminal record. In fact, I remember having a conversation with Mrs. Easterfield several years ago, before I had even heard of Jesse MacIntyre. She told me about the trouble they had with their chef, Alice Brown, stealing from them. I told her that we were very careful about hiring at the club and I'm sure I told her that we would never hire someone with a criminal record, for example. No, I never told Reverend Taylor we would hire someone with a criminal record. He must have misunderstood me.

Yes, there was a rumor around that Mr. Easterfield had been instrumental in the firing of the executive director before me. The rumor was this: The guy was a single fellow who started dating one of the waitresses whom Easterfield himself was seeing. The rumor was that Easterfield had told him to "find himself another girlfriend. Cross me on this and you're through." When he refused, Easterfield had him fired. No reasons. The board just fired him. I called this guy, Arnold Weblow, to check out the rumor and he said he didn't want to talk about it. He said he might need a reference sometime. I did have one dispute with Mr. Easterfield concerning a pay matter, but we resolved it amicably. I ended up with an 8 percent increase when I had been given a 3 percent increase and expected a 10 percent increase. I wrote the letter dated "February 5" during that dispute. It is below at page 127.

Among the officers and members of the club with whom I am associated in the course of my duties, I can say that Mr. Easterfield enjoys the highest reputation for honesty, integrity, and fair dealing. I never believed the rumor about Mr. Arnold Weblow. In my dealings with him, I have always found him to be completely truthful and an honest man to deal with. I would believe him under any circumstances, whether under oath or not.

The deposition was concluded and Marlow was excused.

This deposition was transcribed, and then it was signed by the Deponent, Lee Marlow.

Certified by

A. Marie Lane
_____
Certified Shorthand Reporter (CSR)
Nita City, Nita

EXERCISE 6
FRUITS AND INSTRUMENTALITIES AND OTHER PROBLEMS OF DISCOVERY

You represent Joe Mitchell. Joe made bail three weeks ago. This morning you received a call from him. He asked if he could come in to see you this afternoon and you invited him in.

Soon after the case began you received a standard discovery request from the state. *Inter alia*, the request demands that you turn over "all physical objects in your custody in any way related to the events that are the subject of the indictment" and "all written records of any statement pertaining to the subject of the indictment of any person who has personal knowledge of the events that are the subject of this indictment or who will be or may be a witness in this cause." The request further requires you to identify any such objects or writings of which you are aware but which are not in your possession. You have a continuing obligation to supplement your answers to the request.

You know that written and oral communications from a client to a lawyer made for the purpose of obtaining legal advice are privileged. They need not be revealed in discovery nor may they be presented at trial over the objection of the client. On the other hand, documents, such as diaries or other notes, created by a client for his or her own benefit, are subject to discovery.

★ ★ ★ ★ ★

ASSIGNMENTS:

(A)   Interview Joe Mitchell. Discuss with your fellow interviewer any issues that the interview raises. Announce and explain to the class how you will resolve those issues.

(B)   Identify any violations of the Model Rules you believe the plaintiff's lawyers committed. Be prepared to justify your views.

(C)   Defend the interviewers for any alleged violations of the rules.

(D)   Serve as the disciplinary committee. Hear the arguments of counsel and render a decision on any issues presented. If there has been a violation, determine an appropriate penalty.

Exercises & Problems in Professional Responsibility

Exercises & Problems in Professional Responsibility

EXERCISE 7
NEGOTIATION

This exercise requires students first to interview and counsel their clients, Jesse MacIntyre and Ross Easterfield, concerning a possible settlement of the case of *MacIntyre v. Easterfield*. The students will then negotiate the case, while further counseling their clients during the course of negotiations.

Negotiators will be assigned disciplinary counsel who will "shadow" them throughout the exercise. (This will give disciplinary counsel an unusual degree of knowledge concerning the student-lawyer's conduct of counseling and negotiations.) One of the shadow counsel will serve as prosecutor and the other as defense counsel in the disciplinary hearing that will follow the negotiation. Faculty may play the part of senior partners at the negotiators' firm.

The remaining students will serve as the disciplinary panel. They will also be divided so that half may watch each counseling session. All will be present for the actual negotiations.

Separate background instructions concerning the case will be provided to plaintiff's and defendant's counsel. Both sets of instructions will be provided to disciplinary counsel and the students serving as the disciplinary panel so that they may properly evaluate the student-lawyers' performances. (That is, both sets will be provided to everyone except the lawyers representing the parties in the negotiation who will receive only their own instructions and not those of their opponents.)

* * * * * * * *

ASSIGNMENTS:

(A)   Plaintiff's lawyers will interview and counsel Jesse MacIntyre concerning the possible settlement of the case. They will then conduct a preliminary negotiation with the defendant's lawyers. Plaintiff's lawyers will then conduct yet another counseling session with Jesse and finally seek to negotiate a final agreement with the defense counsel, consulting with Jesse as necessary.

(B)   Defendant's lawyers will interview and counsel Ross Easterfield concerning the possible settlement of the case. They will then conduct a preliminary negotiation with the plaintiff's lawyers. Defendant's lawyers will then conduct yet another counseling session with Easterfield and finally seek to negotiate a final agreement with the plaintiff's counsel, consulting with Easterfield as necessary.

(C)   Identify any violations of the Model Rules you believe the plaintiffs lawyers committed. Be prepared to justify your views.

(D)   Defend the plaintiff's counsel for any alleged violations of the Model Rules.

(E)   Identify any violations of the Model Rules of Professional Conduct you believe the defendant's lawyers committed. Be prepared to justify your views.

(F)   Defend the defendant's counsel for any alleged violations.

(G) Serve as the disciplinary committee. Hear the arguments of counsel and render a decision on any issues presented. If there has been a violation, determine an appropriate penalty.

EXERCISE 8
CROSS-EXAMINATION: IMPEACHMENT

In this exercise defense lawyers will do a portion of the cross-examination of Brooke Thompson. Assume for purposes of this exercise that Joe told you that he committed the killing at 9:45 on September 10. Additionally, he told you that he noticed that the mantel clock in the Thompson home was fifteen minutes fast when he visited the house earlier on the day Leslie was killed, but that he had nothing to do with its running fast.

Assume that Brooke Thompson has testified in a manner consistent with her earlier testimony. [Her testimony from the first trial is attached.] You may use anything in the first transcript in order to conduct the cross-examination. Additionally, for the purposes of this exercise, assume your investigator obtained the attached statement from Brooke (Attachment I) and submitted it to you along with a report (Attachment II).

Assume, too, that you had a conversation with Brooke yesterday on the first floor of the courthouse. You were alone and she walked up to you and asked you whether you were defending Joe Mitchell. She then said to you, "I don't care whether that son-of-a-bitch killed Leslie or not. He deserves to fry just for ruining her life while they were married." You were stunned and tried to get her to continue the conversation, but she said, "That's all I have to say to you. If you quote me, I'll deny it. Who would believe a lawyer?"

In Nita, it is clear that a witness's past acts of theft which involve stealth are available for impeachment. Extrinsic evidence of those acts (that is, evidence other than the witness's own admission of the theft on cross) is not admissible.

Cross-examine Brooke Thompson solely on the events of September 10 and on her credibility as a witness.

Jean Peterson, your investigator, died suddenly of a heart attack three weeks ago. It is quite clear that her report is inadmissible.

* * * * * * *

ASSIGNMENTS:

(A) Conduct the cross-examination of Brook Thompson.

(B) Identify any violations of the Model Rules of Professional Conduct you believe the lawyers committed. Be prepared to defend your views.

(C) Defend the cross-examiner for any alleged violations of the rules.

(D) Serve as the disciplinary committee. Hear the arguments of counsel and render a decision on any issues presented. If there has been a violation, determine an appropriate penalty.

Exercises & Problems in Professional Responsibility

Statement of Brooke Thompson
(Attachment I)

I was not wearing my glasses when I went to the door of my house at 10 P.M. on September 10. They are for distance. I have rather striking blue eyes, my best feature. One cannot really appreciate them when I have my glasses on and one never knows who is going to drop in to visit.

When I saw Mitchell reach out of the car window, I was sure it was him. I have a clear picture of him. He was wearing a jacket, one of those tan poplin jackets that middle-aged men wear. He was also wearing a dark baseball cap with a brim.

I was taking prescribed drugs on that day. I was taking an antidepressant, Conzac. I was also taking estrogen, which I have taken for twelve years. I was using a cortisone suppository for hemorrhoids. I always take five vitamin pills in the morning: a betacarotin pill, a vitamin E pill, a vitamin C pill, a vitamin D pill, and a multivitamin. I also take iron and zinc pills each morning. My doctor has discouraged this, but I don't think that the medical profession can be trusted on "alternative medicine." I see an acupuncturist once every two weeks and a chiropractor once a week. None of these pills damage my ability to perceive. Indeed, they sharpen it.

I had five drinks around dinner time that night, two Manhattans before dinner and three glasses of wine with dinner. I have had some trouble with alcohol over the years, but I am not an alcoholic.

The judge was my fifth husband. Three died of natural causes and I was divorced from two.

I ___ ow a pacifist and I hate guns. That time when I had to kill a ma___ ___ ___y eyes. I strongly disapproved of Mitchell's interest in ___ ___ion with, guns. As a pacifist, I abhor our u___ ___ ___ Iraq. I tried to contribute to Saddam ___ ___ ___ make up for some of the harm we have done, ___ ___ it was illegal to do that and my check was

___ ___ you think you saw at the City Foundry. I never vi___ ___ er Leslie's death.

I have neve_ stolen anything in my entire life.

Exercises & Problems in Professional Responsibility

Exercises & Problems in Professional Responsibility

Investigator's Report
(Attachment II)

My name is Jean Peterson and I am a licensed private investigator. I have worked as a PI since I retired from the Nita Police, where I had worked for twenty years. For the last twelve years on the force, I worked as a detective.

I investigated the death of Leslie Thompson for Joe Mitchell's attorney. I discovered a few things of interest.

I placed Brooke Thompson under surveillance beginning three days after Leslie's death. One day I tailed her to the Nita City Foundry. She walked up to an observation deck up over one of the vats of molten iron. They allow the public up there to view the steelmaking process. There's a very high fence in front of the deck, too high, and with small slits so that it is virtually impossible to climb. They are probably wary of suicides, I suppose. I saw Brooke Thompson look around furtively and then throw a gun over the fence and into the vat.

I continued to tail Brooke Thompson that day. After she left the Foundry, she drove over to the T-Mart on Grove Street. I could not believe my eyes. She shoplifted three or four garments from the store. She did it so furtively that none of the store security people noticed.

I am preparing this report twelve days after the events it describes at the direction of Joseph Mitchell's counsel.

Exercises & Problems in Professional Responsibility

Exercises & Problems in Professional Responsibility

BROOKE THOMPSON'S TESTIMONY

BROOKE L. THOMPSON, called to testify as a witness for the State and having been duly sworn, testified as follows:

My name is Mrs. Brooke L. Thompson. I live at 1751 Madison Street, Nita City, Nita. I am forty-nine years old. I am a widow. My husband, Henry J. Thompson, died on October 1, YR-14. We had no children. I married him in YR-22. It was my first marriage and his second. His first wife died in YR-24. They had one child, Leslie, who was six years old when I married him. Leslie was my stepdaughter. My husband had been a prominent lawyer in Nita City and then, during the first year we were married, he was appointed judge for the circuit court here in Nita City. He was a judge until he died.

When I married Mr. Thompson, he owned the house at 1751 Madison. I have lived there ever since. Of course, Leslie, my stepdaughter, lived there, too, until she married Joe Mitchell. In his will, my husband left all his property to me for my life, and then to Leslie, when I die. The will provided that if Leslie were to die before me, I could dispose of the property as I see fit. The will also set up a trust fund for Leslie and me, with the Nita National Bank and Trust Company as trustee. I was also named Leslie's guardian until she was twenty-one. Her father's estate had given me an income of $25,000 a year on the average, mainly from stocks, bonds, and other investments. Because of poor investment decisions, my income sank to $18,000 per year in YR-4. I had a life insurance policy on Leslie for $300,000. I was the beneficiary, and the policy has paid off, double indemnity. So I received $600,000 on it a couple months after she died. The double indemnity provision included homicides, unless, of course, the beneficiary was the killer.

I needed to supplement my income, so in YR-3, on the recommendation of a real estate agent, I bought two apartment buildings in a rather unpleasant part of Nita City. All the residents were minorities: about twenty-four families—or what they call "families," anyway. The real estate guy said I was in a good position to have a steady income because the judges knew I was a judge's widow and would be "attentive to my concerns" in any building court cases. Those cases are a big problem for landlords in those neighborhoods. I had a management company run the buildings, but I insisted on collecting the rents myself. You have to lay down the law to those people. The tenants, I mean. So I went over there on the first of the month and collected the rents myself; no "ifs," "ands," or "buts." If they didn't have the rent right there in cash or money order, I just phoned in the names and began eviction proceedings. Even if they came up with the money the day after, that was just too bad. It's important to maintain your credibility. I carried my .38 and it was a good thing, too. Once this guy came at me with a knife and I shot him right in the chest. Justifiable homicide, the police said. They also told me I was crazy to collect the rents in those buildings myself. But it hasn't stopped me.

Leslie and I lived comfortably on Madison Street. Although I never formally adopted her as my daughter, I always regarded her as mine. I loved her and took care of her upbringing as if she were my own child. She was so young, only four, when her own mother died that she could hardly remember her. She called me "Mother," and our relations were always the intimate relations of mother and daughter. I was interested in her welfare and in her future happiness and always wanted to advise her as her mother.

I supported Leslie, sent her to school, and raised her. For high school, she went to Greenwood Academy, a private boarding school for girls in Jackson City, Nita. She graduated from there in YR-10. Then, because she didn't want to go to college, I sent her to the Katherine Gibbs Business School in New York in YR-6. She came back to Nita City and got a job at the First State Bank. At the time of her death, she was private secretary to Mr. Robert Allen, the president, and making $1,500 a month. Of course, when she married she was also getting about $500 a month from the trust fund under the terms of the trust document. I receive that now. Leslie's trust contained the provision that I would maintain title to the principal until she was married for four continuous years. Thereafter, she gained control of the principal to do with as she wished. She lived at home with me before her marriage, and all the trust income came to me to use for our benefit as I saw fit. I charged her only market rates for room and board and for household expenses and never asked her to contribute to the maintenance of the house. I knew I could have charged more but I didn't want to—I loved her as my own child.

Late in YR-4, she began to date Joe Mitchell. She brought him home one night and introduced him to me. When I asked him what he did for a living, he said he was a "writer" of short stories and TV scripts, especially detective stories and murder mysteries. He told me he hadn't sold or placed any of his writing yet. In fact, he hadn't made a cent out of it. But he said he was working as a part-time attendant at a gas station to support himself. He said he was then living at Mrs. Porter's boarding house at 800 Fillmore Avenue in Nita City.

I didn't like this man, I admit, and as Leslie continued to date him, my dislike of him increased. I never approved of him. I didn't think he would make Leslie happy if she married him. I warned her against marrying him; I thought it was my duty to her as her mother. I told her I thought he was lazy and shiftless, and would ruin her life. I told her she should date other young men and that she would find she could do better than marrying this fellow. And as it has turned out, my judgment about him was right.

In the winter and spring of YR-3, Mitchell came to our house many times. He dated Leslie three or four times a week. She told me that she had to pay for the gas for the car, and for the dinners and shows they went to, because "Joe was short of money." I guess she sort of pitied him.

In spite of all I did to prevent it, Leslie told me in the summer YR-3 that she was going to marry Joe. I wondered how he expected to support a wife. From what I saw, he was going to live on her money. I told her many times I didn't think Joe was the man for her and that her own father and mother, if they were alive, wouldn't approve of this marriage. I disliked Joe the more I saw of him. From what I saw of him while he was dating Leslie, I thought he was a lazy good-for-nothing. (I admit I never had much use for "writers" anyway.) I was convinced that he'd break her heart. I thought it was my duty to warn her as her own mother would have, that this man would never make her happy. I said he was lazy and was just after what little money she had or could expect. But she became defiant and said she was over twenty-one and they would be married, no matter what I or anyone else said. She said she loved Mitchell. This was the first disagreement we ever had. I was heartbroken. I would have done anything to prevent the marriage. If only I had, she would be alive today. But they went ahead and were married by a judge in Nita City on November 15, YR-3. I wasn't present, because I was ill. I did not want to do anything to suggest that I was approving of what they had done, so I sent no wedding gift.

After their marriage, Joe and Leslie lived in an apartment at 50 Jackson Street. Leslie continued to work at the bank, but Joe quit his job at the gas station so he could stay home and devote all his time to his writing. Leslie was supporting them both. That's just what I expected would happen.

After they were married, they came to my house a couple of times a month, and I was always civil to Mitchell. He admitted he was not making a dime from his writing. They used to come in Mitchell's old white Pontiac. I don't know why Leslie didn't buy a new car. She could drive. She had money, and Mitchell would park the car at the curb right out in front of the house. I had seen it there many times before the night he shot Leslie.

Sometime in late July, YR-2, Leslie came home one night in a taxi. She and Mitchell had separated after a bitter argument. She said she had tried to get Joe to give up his writing and take a job at the bank, but he had refused. I told her I was glad to have her back home without Joe and that she certainly could live with me.

After they separated, Leslie lived with me, and Mitchell went back to live at Porter's boarding house on Fillmore Street. Mitchell would come to the house about twice a week and argue with Leslie to get her to come back to him. She always refused to unless he quit his writing and got a "real" job. I was always present during these arguments. I didn't trust him; I was also afraid that with all his smooth talk, he would get her to go back. So I insisted on being present. After all, it was my house and it was my duty to watch out for her welfare as her mother. I didn't want to see her heart broken any more than it was already. I told her not to go back to him and urged her to consider divorcing him.

Several times, I told Mitchell in very plain language what I, Leslie's mother, thought of it all. I told him he was lazy and no good to be living off his wife's income. We had bitter words in Leslie's presence, and a couple of times he threatened me. He said something about getting even with me because I had broken up his marriage to Leslie. (I am not sure of his exact words, but that's what he meant.) And several times, he threatened to hurt me or Leslie for ruining his marriage. This man had a violent temper. Sometimes he would try to coax Leslie to come back to him; other times he would fly into a rage.

One time in late August, YR-2, he was at the house arguing with Leslie and got angry and rushed out of the house. He slammed the front door so hard I thought it was smashed. I ran to the door and opened it, and saw him run down the walk. I saw him get into his car at the curb across the street. I could see him clearly, even though it was about 9:30 P.M. and dark and raining. I watched him get into the car, and then, before he drove away, I saw him lean out of the car window and shake his fist at me. I was standing at the door, and I could easily see him and recognize his face—pale and sort of drawn.

As I said, he had an uncontrollable temper. When he came to see Leslie, he would shout and scream and say that she was "heartless" and "selfish," and he'd turn on me and accuse me of breaking up his marriage. A couple of times he swore and cursed at us. Then he'd storm out of house, but a few days later he'd be back, and the same things would happen again. Leslie would never leave the house with him. He would ask her to go with him "to talk things over" where I couldn't be around. She would never do it; she was afraid of him, she said. When she told me that, I told her never to leave the house with him. I was really afraid then that he would do some violence to her.

The last time he visited her before he killed her was on September 9, YR-2. I was present. He didn't quarrel with her then, and he only stayed a little while between 9:00 and 10 P.M. He asked her to come back to him. He said: "Leslie, I'm asking you for the last time. You'd better listen to me now, if you know what's good for you." And she said: "Joe, I'm not coming back until you get a real job and quit this silly stuff about writing." He said: "You know I won't do that. I'm not giving up my work, even for you." She said: "Then this is the way it's got to be. I'm all through with you, Joe. I'm sorry it worked out like this." Then Joe said: "Well, I guess there's no use trying anymore, the way you feel. I won't bother you again. But don't forget this—I'm going to make you regret what you've done to me, if it's the last thing I ever do." Leslie then said, "Are you threatening me?" And he just looked at her real mean and angry. Then he said to me: "You are an evil person. You turned Leslie against me. You broke up this marriage, and I'll see that you pay for this. You'll be to blame for whatever happens now." I cannot swear to the exact words used that night, but I do remember the substance of what each said. Mitchell left the house at about 9:30 P.M. Just before he left the house, Joe went into the next room to get his jacket. While he was gone, I said to Leslie, "That man's a loser. I'd rather die than see you go back to him." At that moment, he came back into the room and glowered at me. I think he heard me and it made me nervous.

Yes, I did own a Smith and Wesson .38 caliber revolver, which I bought a few years ago. It was registered. I kept it in the drawer of the night table next to my bed in my bedroom on the first floor of the house. I last saw it on the first or second day of September when I happened to be looking in the drawer. Joe had seen me put the gun in that drawer several times. I looked in the drawer a couple of days after Leslie's death and it was empty. I didn't say anything to the police about its disappearance because I didn't think it was that important. I mentioned it only when the detective asked me if I owned a .38 and whether they could see it. That was about three weeks after Leslie's death. Frankly, I think Joe took it. The gun they recovered from Joe was not mine.

The next day, September 10, was Leslie's birthday. We had dinner at 6 P.M., and I gave her a ring for a present. At about 7 P.M., she left the house to go to a movie at the Palace Theater. She said she would be home around 10 P.M. She went alone. The theater is on Madison Street, about five blocks east, and she walked. It wasn't raining then, but she took an umbrella with her. It was a warm sort of fall evening. After she left, I went upstairs. I noticed that she had left the light on in her room—the front bedroom on the east side of the house. I went in to turn it off, and I noticed she had left her front-door key on the night table. I also saw a piece of paper with some handwriting on it, but I didn't read it then. I decided to wait up for her, since she had forgotten her key.

At 7:30 P.M., the front doorbell rang. I went to answer and opened the door. It was raining then, but just a drizzle. I saw Mitchell standing on the porch. His car, that old white Pontiac, was parked at the south curb across the street, facing east. He asked for Leslie. I told him she had gone to the Palace Theater. He wanted to know when she'd be home, but I said I wasn't sure. I told him this because I didn't want him bothering her again after what he'd said last night—he had said that he wouldn't see her again. I was afraid for her. (I expect that he knew that Leslie almost always went to Heggarty's after seeing a show and almost always stayed until 12:30 A.M. or so. Heggarty's is one of those beer, burger, and ice cream places where neighborhood young people gather. Nice quiet place a couple blocks east of the Palace.) He spoke clearly and calmly. He had something under his right arm. It was wrapped in an old newspaper, and I couldn't tell what it was. He was wearing a sort of black or dark blue jacket.

Around 10 P.M., the doorbell rang again. I went and opened the door. (It opens in.) Leslie was there. She was standing on the porch about two or three feet from the step. The bracket lights at the door were on. I also had the lights on in the two front rooms on the first floor, and the window drapes were open.

Leslie had her back to the street. It was raining and dark—cloudy and no moonlight; there was no streetlight at the curb. But there was a streetlight at the south curb, across the street, thirty feet west of my front door.

Just then, I heard a car coming from the west and going east on Madison. There were no other cars on the street. I looked out and saw a white car—it was a Pontiac, same style and shape as Mitchell's. You see, I had the door open, and I looked out over Leslie's head as she stood down on the porch. The car came on fast, going east. All of a sudden I heard the brakes squeal, and the car stopped out at the curb right in front of our house.

I suddenly realized this was Mitchell's car, and then Leslie cried out, "Oh no . . . oh no, Joe!" or something like that. It all happened in a matter of seconds. I saw a man lean out of the car window—put his head and shoulders out of the front window on the side facing us. He didn't have a hat on. I saw a small, dark object in his hand, like a gun or some kind of revolver. Then I heard a shot—only one shot—and I saw Leslie fall over backwards. She sort of spun around and fell on the porch, with her head towards the street and her feet in the direction of the door. The car sped away down the street, going east. I saw the taillights, but I couldn't see the license plate number. The motor or engine of this car was running through the whole thing—I could hear it all the time the car was stopped at the curb.

The first thought that flashed in my mind was that Joe had shot my daughter. I can positively swear that the face of the man who leaned out of the car was the face of Joe Mitchell and that it was his car. I saw his face. I saw the car. I know it was Joe Mitchell. As I told you, I had seen Mitchell hundreds of times before, right out there at the curb in that car—the white Pontiac. And I had seen him there only three hours before. I'm not identifying a stranger I had seen on the night of the murder for the first time; I had seen Mitchell hundreds of times. I knew him; he was no stranger. And I recognized the car, too.

Joe Mitchell is definitely the man I saw fire the shot from the car. I saw his face for a couple of seconds, but that was enough. Leslie was not blocking my view; she was only five-foot, two inches, and was standing down on the porch, while I was on the step at the door, about one foot up from the porch. Leslie had an umbrella and was just closing it, but she had it down when she turned and faced the street.

The two porch lights were on and there was light from the two front room windows. The car had its headlights on. No, there wasn't any moonlight. It was dark and raining—not hard, but there was rain splashing on the porch.

Some neighbors came running over right away and took me into the house. I was in shock. Some police came, but I don't know who called them. One of the police officers—I can't remember his name now—asked me some questions, and I told him pretty much what I've told you. I told him Leslie's husband was Joe Mitchell and he lived at Porter's boarding house at 800 Fillmore Avenue. I said that Joe Mitchell had shot and killed his wife, Leslie, my stepdaughter. When the ambulance came to take Leslie to the hospital, I rode along, and a doctor there pronounced her dead on arrival. Then I had to identify Leslie's body to a man who said he was the coroner.

I'm sure it was 10 P.M. when Leslie came home from the Palace Theater, because just as she rang the doorbell, I heard my clock in the living room strike ten.

I only saw Mitchell out there in the car for a few seconds, but saw the car for a longer time. I saw it coming for about four or five seconds before it stopped. Then I saw Mitchell lean out of the window, take aim, and shoot Leslie.

September 10 was Leslie's birthday. When Mitchell came to the house earlier that night asking for Leslie, he didn't say anything to me about her birthday. The package he had under his arm was large enough to conceal a pistol or handgun. He didn't have a hat or an umbrella, and his jacket was soaked with rain.

One day while Mitchell and Leslie were dating, he came to the house to see Leslie, and he had a handgun with him. He said he had been out target shooting with the gun. He claimed he was an expert shot.

After Leslie's funeral, I was in her room and I remembered the piece of paper I had seen on her night table the night she was shot. I looked at it then, and it was a letter to Leslie from Joe. I recognized the handwriting—it is Joe Mitchell's handwriting. I had seen him sign our guestbook once, and I've seen his handwriting on his letters to Leslie. The handwriting on the letter is the same as the handwriting on the guestbook and the letters.

I remember that on the morning of September 10, a letter came special delivery for Leslie. I recognized Mitchell's handwriting on the envelope. (No, I have never found this envelope.) I gave Leslie the letter when she came home. That night at dinner, she said the letter was from him. She never said what was in it, and we never discussed this.

There's one other thing maybe I should mention, although I'm sure there's no connection. My husband, Leslie's father, had been a judge for several years before his death. He handled some notorious criminal trials, and I'm sure along the way he made some enemies, particularly some of those he sentenced. I remember one case especially, because I read in the newspaper last August that the person my husband had sentenced had been paroled and was returning to Nita City. That case involved a fairly well-known businessman who was convicted for killing his business associate. There was a lot of publicity and talk of connections with gambling and organized crime. My husband was under a lot of pressure at the trial and sentencing. He said he had to do his duty and do what the law required. The jury found the man—I think his name is John Bierman—guilty, and my husband sentenced him to something like twenty-five to thirty years in prison. This was all about fifteen years ago, just a couple of years before my husband died. At the sentencing, Bierman said he was innocent and had been framed by my husband and the prosecutor. My husband said in his remarks from the bench that he had talked the sentence over with "my wife" and was sure it was fair. I wish he had not said that. Bierman said he'd get revenge "on you and your goddamned wife" for having his life ruined and losing his family in a frame-up if it was the last thing he did. My husband and I were concerned about this threat at the time, and I remember him talking about it for some time. I also remember that Bierman had a wife and three children, and that she divorced him and left town shortly after he went to prison. Naturally, he lost his business when he went to prison.

CERTIFICATION BY COURT REPORTER

The above is a true and accurate transcription of (Mrs.) Brooke Thompson's testimony at the trial of the case of *State v. Mitchell*, which testimony was recorded stenographically by me at the time it was given.

Signed and Attested to by:

a Marie Lane

Certified Court Reporter

Exercises & Problems in Professional Responsibility

EXERCISE 9
CROSS-EXAMINATION: THE TRUTHFUL WITNESS

In this exercise, counsel for the defendant will conduct a cross-examination of Mary Stuart.

Assume that Joe told you that he did not shoot his wife and you believe him completely. You are impressed with the genuineness of his grief over his wife's death, his earnestness in maintaining that he would never harm Brooke despite his animosity toward her, and the consistency over a long period of his story about what happened on the night of September 10. [His description of what occurred on September 10, as he testified at his first trial, is attached.]

Assume further that Joe was once convicted of aggravated assault in connection with an angry shooting at a motorist who made an obscene gesture toward him. The court has made a pretrial ruling that the shooting is inadmissible under Rule 404(b) but will be admissible under Rule 609, if Joe testifies. This is one reason you and Joe have decided it is best that he not testify.

There is another reason. Joe told you that he did in fact leave Mrs. Porter's boarding house after she saw him come in at 9:55 P.M. He felt dejected after reading a letter rejecting one of his scripts and thought he needed some air. He walked down the front stairs of the boarding house and walked out the front door. He walked for about twenty-five minutes in the rain and then returned, again walking up the front stairs. He didn't see Mrs. Porter either on the way in, or the way out, and apparently she did not see him. A few minutes after he returned, the police arrived.

If you don't call Joe, you intend to maintain that the evidence does not suggest that he ever saw the rejection letter. Further, you can rely heavily on the near impossibility of Joe's returning to the boarding house as late as 9:55 and then shooting Leslie and being back at the boarding house at 10:30.

If Joe takes the stand and testifies to what actually happened, he will provide the prosecution with a strong motive (his dejection) and destroy your best theory of the case.

There is one major problem with your strategy. Two weeks after Leslie's death, Mary Stuart came forward and claimed to have seen Joe on the street near the boarding house at 10:15 P.M. Joe tells you that he remembers seeing Mary Stuart on the street at 10:15, on his way in the second time. He is quite certain it was the second time because of the location of where he was when Stuart saw him.

Stuart's testimony is weak for a number of reasons, which are apparent from the attached statement. Joe is actually six-foot, two inches-tall, and weighs 200 pounds. He has blond hair. The wet clothes that the police recovered were a dark jacket and a pair of blue jeans. After Stuart failed to identify Joe in a line-up, the police showed her a single photograph, that of Joe Mitchell, and she told them that this was the man whom she had seen. She has poor vision without her glasses and she was not wearing her glasses that evening.

Nonetheless, you believe from what Joe has told you that she did indeed see Joe Mitchell at 10:15 P.M. on September 10.

Assume that Mary Stuart has just testified on direct. On direct, she testified that she saw the defendant, for whom she provided an in-court all identification, on the street near Mrs. Porter's at 10:15 P.M. on the night Leslie was killed. She did not include the other information in her statement.

* * * * * * * *

ASSIGNMENTS:

(A) Conduct the cross-examination of Mary Stuart.

(B) Identify any violations of the Model Rules you believe the lawyers committed. Be prepared to defend your views.

(C) Defend the cross-examiner for any alleged violations of the rules.

(D) Serve as the disciplinary committee. Hear the arguments of counsel and render a decision on any issues presented. If there has been a violation, determine an appropriate penalty.

STATEMENT

My name is Mary Stuart and I work at a battered women's shelter here in Nita City. On the evening of September 10, I was on my way home from work. I had stopped off for a few drinks with friends. I had perhaps four bourbons over a period of an hour.

I was waiting for my bus at the corner of Fillmore and Sak streets when I saw a man I now know to be Joe Mitchell. He was about five-foot, eight inches-tall, and about 160 pounds. He had dark hair and was wearing grey slacks and a tan jacket. He was walking north on Filmore Street. I know it was 10:15 because it was moments before I caught the 10:15 bus and that bus is always on time. Buses run every fifteen minutes. I think it was the 10:15 because the bus trip takes about ten minutes and I had been home about a half hour when I first looked at the clock. The clock said 11 P.M.

I saw the newspaper reports of Leslie's death on September 11. They made me think about how terrible the violence against women is in our society. There was a picture of Joe Mitchell in the paper and he kind of looked familiar, but I didn't think anything of it.

I thought about the case often over the next two weeks. Two weeks later there was another story in the paper about the case. Mitchell's lawyer said to a reporter that he had already returned to his boarding house by the time of the killing, 10 P.M., and gave the address of the boarding house. There was another picture of Mitchell in that paper. The more I looked at the picture, the surer I became that Mitchell was the man I had seen at 10:15 P.M.

I called the police department and they told me to come in for a line up. They held a line up in which I now know Joe Mitchell was one of the subjects. I told them that I could not identify anyone. They then showed me one photograph of Joe Mitchell and I told them that this was the man I saw at 10:15.

Signed: _Mary Stuart_

Exercises & Problems in Professional Responsibility

Exercises & Problems in Professional Responsibility

EXCERPT FROM JOE MITCHELL'S TESTIMONY

September 10 was Leslie's birthday. I cashed my check and bought a five-pound box of candy. I wanted to see Leslie to tell her about my good luck and maybe get her to come back after all. The box of candy was for her birthday. I went back to the boarding house and paid Mrs. Porter some back rent and board.

That night I drove to 1751 Madison Street in my car, a used YR-12 Pontiac Ventura I've had for a couple of years. I wanted to surprise Leslie. I got to 1751 Madison at about 7:30 P.M., but I'm not positive about the time.

I parked at the south curb across the street from 1751 Madison, with my car pointed east. There were two porch lights on brackets on either side of the door, about five feet up from the ground. Both lights were on. Mrs. Thompson came to the door, and I asked for Leslie. She told me that Leslie had gone to the Palace Theater, where Leslie and I had often gone. I asked when she would be back, and Mrs. Thompson said 10:10 P.M. I thought that was a strangely precise hour. I couldn't quite describe her manner. It was strange, like the witch in Hansel and Gretel: trying to be sweet, but kind of rubbing her hands together. Being nice doesn't become her. Anyway, she said that if I wanted to talk with Leslie I should come back at exactly 10:10 and come alone. I did not tell Mrs. Thompson about having sold the TV script. I only talked to her for a few minutes at the most. She did not ask me in, of course; it was raining, and she made me just stand there in the rain. I didn't have a hat or an umbrella, and I was getting pretty wet. I had the box of candy under my arm. I hadn't wanted the wrapping to get wet, so I wrapped it in a couple of newspapers.

I left Mrs. Thompson's at about 7:35 P.M. or so, and drove to the Palace Theater. I thought I would try to surprise Leslie there. Since I had just gotten my first check for my writing, I wanted to share it with her. While I was driving there, I was trying to think things out. The idea that I would lose Leslie because of Mrs. Thompson upset me. I couldn't see myself living without her. I was in love with my wife. It seemed so cruel and ironic really that I should lose out by one day after waiting so long. I did not want to go on without Leslie, so I decided to make one more attempt to talk to her. I hoped that with my writing success and without Mrs. Thompson present, we could get back together.

Exercises & Problems in Professional Responsibility

I parked near the theater. I knew the ticket seller there, Quinn Washington. I had met her often when Leslie and I went there, because she was a friend of Leslie's. I think it was about 7:45 P.M. or so when I arrived. The ticket booth is in front of the theater. I went up to the booth and asked her if she had seen Leslie. I told her I had been to Mrs. Thompson's and that Mrs. Thompson had told me that Leslie had gone to the Palace Theater. She told me that Leslie had gone into the theater. I remember asking Quinn several times when the show would be over. I think she said the first show would be over at about 9:40 or 9:45 P.M. We talked for a while. I recall Quinn said something about Leslie being "afraid" of me, or something like that. I told Quinn that there was nothing wrong between Leslie and me, but that it was all Mrs. Thompson's fault. I said that Mrs. Thompson was the "evil" person who had broken up my marriage and that my marriage would be okay if Mrs. Thompson were not in the way.

I bought a ticket and went into the theater. I was going to wait for Leslie. I went into the foyer, waited a while and then went to the men's room. I was thinking about selling my writing that day and how, if it hadn't been for Mrs. Thompson, everything would be perfect and Leslie and I would be sharing the success. I got upset, smoked a couple of cigarettes, and then decided to leave. I went out of the theater and got into my car. I drove further east about four or five blocks. I think it was about 8:30 P.M.—I am sorry I can't be precise about the time—and I went into the Silver Dollar Bar there on the south side of Madison Street, about five blocks from the theater.

I had four glasses of beer at the bar. There were about thirty-five people in there. I talked to the bartender, but I don't know his name. As best as I can remember, I was there for about forty-five minutes.

I talked with the bartender, but he was busy serving all the other customers, so we didn't talk continuously. I did not tell him my name, but I do recall telling him I was a writer of short stories, murder mysteries, and crime stories, for TV and radio. And I did say something about my mother-in-law having broken up my marriage and poisoning my wife's mind against me so much that she had left me. I recall I said that my mother-in-law hated me, and maybe I said I hated her too, for all she had done to me. I was pretty down and depressed at the time. I couldn't get the thought out of my head that we were separated, and now I'd made it with my writing.

After about an hour, I think, I left the Silver Dollar. I was certainly not drunk. I went to my car and sat in it a while before driving off. I can't say exactly how long it was, but I think that I left there at about 9:30 P.M. I was trying to decide whether to go back to the theater or go home. My favorite radio program was due to come on at 10:00. I turned around and drove west on Madison. I passed the theater, but didn't stop; I didn't even look over to the ticket booth as I passed. I went past the house at 1751 Madison Street, and the porch lights and the lights in the two front rooms were on. It was still drizzling rain.

I decided to go pick up my .38 caliber revolver at Ravenna's Gun Shop at 2165 Madison. I had left the gun there for cleaning and some minor repairs about a week before. I found the place still open, so I went in. Chris Ravenna, who is a clerk for his brother, Sam, who owns the shop, was there. Chris got the gun for me, and I paid the bill—$6.50—and left. I was only there for a few minutes. You can check that out with Chris.

I bought this gun when I was in the service, and kept it as a memento of service days. The only time I used it was to practice target shooting on the outskirts of Nita City. Since I was a writer of murder mysteries, and many of them involved guns, I thought I ought to be familiar with guns as part of my business. I used to practice a couple of times a week, shooting at paper targets on a tree. This was my only relaxation or sport. I became an expert shot; I once told Leslie I could hit a dime at a hundred yards. And I probably told other people at some time or other in a bragging way that I could do this. Leslie knew I had the gun. I used to keep it in my closet in an old five-pound candy box. I kept it on a shelf of the closet in the boarding house.

At the beginning of September YR-2, I had some trouble with the safety catch, so I took it to Ravenna's Gun Shop for repair and cleaning. Chris Ravenna returned it to me the night of September 10, as I said. When he gave me the gun, I did not notice that there were two shells or bullets in it. I guess I had left them there in the gun when I took it in for repair, and Ravenna must have taken them out while he was making the repairs and doing the cleaning and then replaced them later. Chris reminded me of them when he gave me the gun, and told me to be careful. I took the shells out of the gun and put them in my pants pocket. I put the gun in my jacket pocket. I got in my car and drove home to 800 Fillmore Avenue. I was never near 1751 Madison Street again that night. Each time I have had the gun repaired on previous occasions, I have taken it to the Nita Gun Club for a test firing right away. I have had the gun repaired three times before. The firing range is open until midnight and is about ten minutes from Ravenna's. No particular reason why I didn't do it that night. My radio program, maybe.

When I got home, I went up to my room on the second floor of Mrs. Porter's boarding house. I took off my wet clothes and got into a bathrobe and pajamas. I sat down to read and listen to a rebroadcast of *The Shadow* on the radio. I listen to it every Saturday at 10:00. I've learned more about mystery writing by listening to those shows than any other way. I had a headache that wouldn't go away, and around 10:15 or 10:30 I went down to Mrs. Porter's to borrow some aspirin. I heard her TV and knocked. She was watching TV in her living room, which is on the first floor, facing the street. She gave me some aspirin, and I went back up to my room.

Around 10:45, I think it was, I heard a knock on my door. I opened the door, and there were two men there in police uniforms. One said that he was Officer Slyviak and he asked me my name. I told him "Joe Mitchell," and I said "What's this all about?" Slyviak said that my wife had been shot. That really shook me up. I asked, "Is she dead?" Officer Slyviak said that they did not know whether she was dead or not, but that she had been taken to the hospital by ambulance.

Officer Slyviak asked me if I would go to Police Headquarters with them, and I said I would gladly do so. I told them that, if they would let me dress, I would go with them and help all I could. I told them that I had been reading and listening to the radio. (I had been sitting in a chair reading, and so the bed was still made up.)

I went to get some dry clothing from my closet. When I came in earlier that night, I had thrown my wet clothing on the floor. As I went to get some clothes from the closet, I noticed my wet jacket on the floor and, right alongside it, my gun. I guess it had fallen out of my pocket when I dropped my jacket on the floor. I had taken the shells out of my pants pocket when I got in and had put them in the dresser drawer.

I saw Officer Slyviak sort of move over to pick up the gun, but I picked it up before he got it. I was afraid I was going to get into trouble because I didn't have the gun registered, so I picked it up. But then I handed it over to the officer. I said "I have nothing to hide, Officer." I handed him the jacket, too. I told him again, "I have nothing to hide. You take them."

The officers did not force me to go with them; they did not arrest me. They asked me to go downtown to headquarters, and I went with them voluntarily. I felt at all times that I was free to go with them or refuse to go with them. Neither of these officers at any time said anything to me about having a lawyer, remaining silent, or that anything I said might be used against me.

I told the officers I had bought the gun while in the service and that I used it for target shooting. I told them I wrote murder mysteries and had to know a lot about guns for my writing.

I finished dressing and went out with them. I went to the station in their police car. They did not force me to do this. A man at the station who said he was Detective Bradley, a homicide detective, told me my wife was dead—dead on arrival at the hospital. Bradley went into a room with Officer Slyviak. While Bradley and Slyviak were in the room together, I was left in an interview room. It got stuffy in there and I decided that I needed a little fresh air. I got up and walked toward the front door. The sergeant sitting at the front desk said to me, "Where the hell do you think you're going?" I said, "To get a little fresh air." At that point Bradley came out of the room where he had been with Slyviak. He told me that I was being arrested for the murder of my wife. He said that I had the right to remain silent, that anything I said might be used against me, and that I had the right to call a lawyer. I signed a form and made a statement. I told them I had absolutely nothing to do with my wife's murder, and I knew nothing about the shooting. I told them what I did that night and how I certainly wasn't near 1751 Madison Street at the time of shooting. I told them I was at Chris Ravenna's Shop and then I went right home. I told them to check this with Chris Ravenna and Mrs. Porter. I went right home from Ravenna's shop; I wasn't near 1751 Madison at 10 P.M., and I certainly didn't shoot my wife.

Exercises & Problems in Professional Responsibility

EXERCISE 10
CHARACTER AND FITNESS

In this exercise, counsel will conduct an interview of a third-year law student at Nita Law School who has a problem that may affect her admission to the bar. Counsel then will conduct a negotiation with the dean of Nita Law School.

You practice in Nita. You have received a call from Pat Kurtis, a third-year law student at your alma mater who wants to talk with you. Pat claims to have a problem that may affect her admission to the Nita bar. You know Pat because she worked as your law clerk last summer. You were pleased with the work Pat did. If your firm could afford to hire another associate, you have no doubt that you would make Pat an offer. Pat attends Nita University School of Law.

The Nita version of Rule 8.1 follows the Model Rule. However, it contains the following additional prohibition:

> A lawyer shall not further the application for admission to the bar of another person known by the lawyer to be unqualified in respect to character, education, or any other relevant attribute.

* * * * *

ASSIGNMENTS:

(A) Interview and counsel Pat Kurtis. To the extent that you may ethically do so, represent her in negotiations with the dean and agree to represent her in formal proceedings. Announce and explain to the class how you will resolve any other issues that emerge from the interview.

(B) As dean of the Nita University Law School, negotiate with Kurtis's lawyer. The dean will receive separate instructions.

(C) Identify any violations of the Model Rules you believe the student-lawyers and the dean may have committed. Be prepared to justify your views.

(D) Defend the student-lawyers and the dean for any alleged violations of the rules.

(E) Serve as the disciplinary committee. Hear the arguments of counsel and render a decision on issues presented. If there has been a violation, determine an appropriate penalty.

EXERCISE 11
CHARACTER AND FITNESS DELIBERATIONS

This exercise will require the class to deliberate concerning a number of candidates' fitness to practice law. The class will be designated as the Character and Fitness Committee. It is their task to deliberate on each case and determine whether the applicant should be admitted to the bar.

On each case a student is assigned to argue for admission and one for denial of the application.

You are to assume that each candidate is otherwise qualified to practice. Nita recognizes the authority of the United States Supreme Court. All other authority is persuasive to the right reason of the Committee, constrained only by the Supreme Court's rulings (should those rulings impose a constraint on right reason!).

CASE NUMBER 1. Argue the admission to the bar of Pat Kurtis, the student who was the subject of Exercise 10.

CASE NUMBER 2. The applicant refused to answer a question put to him by the bar examiners to list every organization to which he belongs. In fact, he belongs to the Teutonic Legions, a white supremacist organization, a fact that he prefers to keep to himself. The organization cannot be said to "advocate the violent overthrow of the United States," because it is too weak to have any definite political agenda. It preaches the superiority of the "white race," and urges its members to arm themselves against a vaguely described "takeover" by "the colored races." Its members find it easy to arm to the teeth without violating local gun laws. Assume the committee has learned from other sources about the applicant's membership. The committee's prosecutor seeks to deny the applicant admission based on the failure to respond to the question and also based on the applicant's membership in the Legions. Argue the admission of the candidate.

CASE NUMBER 3. The applicant's ex-wife files an affidavit opposing his admission to the bar. In the affidavit, she alleges that during the course of her five-year marriage to the applicant, he carried on three affairs with other women. He actively deceived her about his relationships with the first two women. During the fourth year of their marriage, he declared that he wanted to try an "open marriage" and was completely candid about his relationship with the third woman. The applicant admits the allegations. Throughout this entire period, your state has had a criminal statute proscribing adultery, though there has not been a prosecution since 1913. Argue the admission of the candidate.

CASE NUMBER 4. The bar examiners simply asked married applicants to list any intimate relationships they had with persons other than their spouses during the course of their marriages. The applicant refused to answer the question, asserting in an attached memorandum that she viewed the question as "outrageous intrusion into my Constitutionally protected zone of privacy." The state has always had in effect the statute described in the previous case. Argue the admission of the candidate.

CASE NUMBER 5. The candidate's ex-wife claims that he battered her on a regular basis throughout their five-year marriage, which ended three years ago, though she never filed criminal charges. She testified to the beatings before the Character and Fitness committee. The candidate admits that he lost control of himself "too many times," perhaps eight, over the five-year period. Both the applicant and his ex-wife agreed that she suffered painful facial bruises and cuts but that she never sought medical attention for them. He expressed his remorse before the committee and claimed that he was "too immature for marriage" when he married at the age of twenty. Argue the admission of the candidate.

CASE NUMBER 6. Assume same facts as in the previous problem but also assume that the applicant's wife filed three criminal battery complaints during the course of their marriage. The applicant pled guilty to all three and received probation the first two times, and sixty days the third. Argue the admission of the candidate.

CASE NUMBER 7. The applicant's ex-spouse has filed an affidavit alleging that the applicant has been erratic in the payment of child support over the past four years. Twice, it was necessary to bring the applicant back to court in order to obtain payments of past-due amounts. At least ten times, the applicant missed a month or two and then made up the past-due amounts. Once, the applicant's spouse and children were evicted from their house because of these late payments. When the applicant heard of the eviction, applicant uttered a profanity and told spouse to work a second job. Argue the admission of the candidate.

CASE NUMBER 8. The applicant was a high school science teacher for twenty years. During that time, he was a prominent member of the North American Man-Boy Love Association. He wrote a regular column in that organization's periodical and authored a short text that one critic described as a "manual for the seduction of young boys." After he was pressured out of his job at the high school, he decided to pursue a legal career. The state has a statute proscribing sodomy and its statutory rape statute encompasses homosexual acts. May the applicant be denied admission based on his knowing membership in an organization that fosters illegal activity? May the committee ask for the names of any minors with whom the applicant has had sexual relations? If the applicant asserts his Fifth Amendment rights, may the committee use his nonresponse as the basis for a denial of admission? Argue the candidate's admission.

CASE NUMBER 9. The *New York Times* for September 13, 1993, carried the story of James J. Hamm, whose life sentence for a drug-related killing, was recently commuted. He served eighteen years, and was at the time of the story, attending the University of Arizona Law School. The story recounted that Hamm said he was "shaken to my moral core and determined to build a new way of looking at myself and the world." He took every self-improvement class the department offered, earned a college degree *summa cum laude* while he was in prison, and scored in the ninety-sixth percentile in his law boards. Mr. Hamm, the story recounted, believed that his case raised important questions: "What does our society want to do with people who have served their sentences? Do we block them and frustrate them? And what about rehabilitation? Do we believe in it? And how do we accomplish it?"

Hamm was the son of a migrant wheat-cutter. The death of his mother seemed to precipitate an "emotional breakdown." He began selling small amounts of marijuana to college students. He was convicted after firing two bullets into the back of the head of a young man whom he had helped lure into a bogus drug deal in order to rob him of $1,400. Mr. Hamm claimed that the horror of what he had done "shook my mental house down." He declined to assert an insanity defense because, he said, only by acknowledging his guilt, could he be in what the story called "the process of self-discovery and perhaps redemption." One political leader criticized his admission to the law school, arguing that Hamm's "precious seat should go to one of the thousands of applicants who didn't shoot somebody in the head." Argue the admission of the candidate.

* * * * *

ASSIGNMENTS:

(A) Argue in favor of the admission of the designated candidate.

(B) Argue against the admission of the designated candidate.

(C) As the Character and Fitness committee, deliberate on and decide the character and fitness to practice law of the candidates.

EXERCISE 12
THE ETHICS AND LAW OF CLOSING ARGUMENT

In this exercise, a faculty member will deliver a prosecutor's rebuttal argument in the case of *State v. Mitchell*. A number of students will be designated as defense counsel. It will be their responsibility to make the appropriate objections in the course of the closing argument, drawing both on the law of closing argument and the closely related ethical obligations of trial counsel. Objections should, of course, be stated with specificity. Counsel may ask for a sidebar, if necessary, to provide the court a more extended explanation. You should assume that the only evidence presented at trial was the clearly admissible evidence in the case file.

* * * * *

ASSIGNMENTS:

(A) Represent Joe Mitchell during the prosecutor's closing arguments, making the appropriate objections. Decide whether you are permitted or obliged to report the prosecutor to the disciplinary authority for her conduct during closing.

(B) Serve as judge. Make the necessary rulings, stating your grounds each time. Decide whether to refer the prosecutor to the disciplinary authority for her conduct during closing.

Exercises & Problems in Professional Responsibility

Exercises & Problems in Professional Responsibility

EXERCISE 13
CONFLICTS OF INTEREST:
CIVIL

Jesse MacIntyre has come to the law firm of Demetral & Wilson, asking for representation in her suit against Mr. Easterfield. She was interviewed by Ms. Demetral, the firm's senior partner. Ms. Demetral has accepted Jesse's case because she dislikes Mr. Easterfield and because Reverend Taylor told her that if her firm does a good job in this case, the Archdiocese may put the firm on retainer.

Demetral & Wilson is attempting to gain more of a market share of Nita's legal business. The firm is one of the oldest in Nita City, but its leadership has until now, insisted that it remain relatively small—in the forty-to-fifty range. With the retirement of some of the firm's older partners, the younger members of the firm have become determined to catch up with the Nita City firms that expanded during the 1980s. The firm has begun to search for lateral hires in two categories—lawyers who will bring business to the firm and lawyers with extensive litigation experience who can manage the business that will be brought to the firm.

Shortly after the firm accepted Jesse's case, it heard of the availability of Sarah Morgan, a top litigator with the firm of Berry, Moehn, Foley & Madden. Morgan is having a dispute with her partners over her share of the firm's profits. She wants to move on. She sees association with Demetral & Wilson as an interesting, and possibly lucrative, step. Demetral & Wilson has discussed briefly with Morgan the possibility of becoming the head of Demetral's litigation department.

You are one of the younger partners on Demetral's management committee. You are scheduled to interview Ms. Morgan. You have heard that the other members of the management committee are anxious to make this lateral hire. The business brought in by Morgan will make the future of the firm. The purpose of this interview is to satisfy yourself that Ms. Morgan would be a suitable addition to your distinguished firm. The firm's senior partner, (Marianne or Michael) Demetral, will also be present at the interview. One wrinkle is that the Berry firm represents Ross Easterfield in Jesse's case. Sarah Morgan herself, however, has not filed an appearance in the case and seems to have no involvement in it.

* * * * *

ASSIGNMENTS:

(A) Conduct the interview of Ms. Morgan.

(B) Serve on the firm's Management committee. Deliberate and decide those issues, which Ms. Morgan's possibly joining the firm raises.

Exercises & Problems in Professional Responsibility

EXERCISE 14
CONFLICTS OF INTEREST:
CRIMINAL

You represent Joe Mitchell. You have just learned that the police have also arrested John Bierman for the murder of Leslie Thompson. The announcement was made in the newspaper this morning. After reading the newspaper account of Bierman's arrest, which stated that the police recently discovered that Mitchell and Bierman committed the crime together, you receive a call from Joe Mitchell. Joe asks you to come to the Nita County jail as soon as possible. He wants to talk to you about Bierman's arrest. Joe tells you that he has known Bierman for some time. He based one of his crime novels on Bierman's experience with the Nita justice system. Joe also tells you that Bierman needs a lawyer. He plans to arrange to have Bierman with him when you meet at the jail.

* * * * *

ASSIGNMENTS:

(A) Conduct the interview of Mitchell and Bierman.

(B) Identify any violations of the Model Rules you believe the lawyers committed. Be prepared to defend your views.

(C) Defend the interviewers.

(D) Serve as the disciplinary committee. Hear the arguments of counsel and render a decision. If there has been a violation, determine an appropriate penalty.

Exercises & Problems in Professional Responsibility

PROBLEMS

Exercises & Problems in Professional Responsibility

PROBLEM SET A.
CLIENT COUNSELING

1.   Jesse tells you that she is receiving general assistance benefits of $165 per month in addition to the $250 per month she receives as part-time work at the rectory. She tells you that she can barely get by on this $415 per month. She has not reported her earnings to public assistance. She wants to know if she would be eligible for food stamps as well, and whether Public Aid will find out about about her earnings if she applies for food stamps.

    You know that Public Aid is no more likely to find out about her employment because of the application for food stamps. You know, too, that Jesse would be eligible for $120 in stamps if she reports only her general assistance, but only $30 if she includes her earned income from the rectory.

    Speak to Jesse.

2.   Jesse tells you that she has a good job prospect at the Weston House hotel, but that she omitted her job with the Easterfields from her list of previous employers. She tells you that Reverend Taylor is willing to say that she worked at the rectory since she got out of prison. (Taylor says, "Some things are more important than literal truth.")

    She tells you that she needs your help to get an original of her birth certificate in order to get the job because she is a resident alien. She tells you she knows that the bureaucrats back in Ireland will move much more quickly if they know that she is represented by an attorney and asks that you write a cover letter for the affidavit she must submit in order to get the birth certificate. The cover letter would merely make the request for the birth certificate.

    What should you do?

3.   Jesse met a young man with whom she has fallen in love. After a three-month courtship, they have decided to live together. Unfortunately, Jesse is still legally married to someone whom she married in Las Vegas a week after she got out of prison. (They lived together for two weeks and she hasn't seen him in over a year.) According to a statute passed in 1884 and last enforced in 1937, adultery is a criminal offense in Nita.

    May you negotiate with Jesse's landlord on her behalf for favorable terms for her lease?

4.   Jesse tells you that she wants you to represent her in a divorce action against her husband. The state recognizes abandonment, physical cruelty, mental cruelty and adultery as grounds for divorce. You know that mental cruelty requires that the defendant criticize or deliberately embarrass the plaintiff publicly, at least twice. Jesse tells you that this didn't happen.

    If she wants a divorce now, she will have to testify to "grounds" during what the judges refer to as "perjury hour," the time at which uncontested divorces are "proven up." If she doesn't have "grounds" she will have to wait until she has lived apart from her husband for two years.

    Explain to Jesse what you will do.

5.   Even though Jesse is not seeking alimony, court rules require that each spouse file a copy of the previous year's tax return attached to her pleadings. (The court might want to order alimony for the defendant.) You know that Jesse failed to report her general assistance benefits on the return as she was required to, and therefore received $800 too much in earned income tax credit.

    May you file the divorce pleadings, including the tax return? If you may not, is Jesse doomed never to be divorced?

Exercises & Problems in Professional Responsibility

6. You are a staff attorney for the Women's Law Center and you handle a range of cases involving reproductive rights and domestic violence. One afternoon, two women from a "subgroup" of the American Organization for Women appear at your office. You have talked with them once or twice briefly at political meetings. They tell you that they have planned a "counterdemonstration" to oppose an Operation Rescue action in the city. One of them hands you ten thousand dollars in cash and asks you if you will "hold on to it and use it for bail money, if necessary." They also ask you if you will represent them in any criminal matters that may arise from the counterdemonstration.

     Your answer?

7. Assume that Jesse MacIntyre has come to your office for the first time a week after leaving the Easterfields. Assume she tells you that she did, in fact, take the brooch from Mrs. Easterfield's dresser and has it in her purse. She wants to return it to the Easterfields "to get this mess behind me." She has asked Kelly Emerson to place it discretely in the library so it will look like Mrs. Easterfield left it there.

     "Should I go ahead with that plan?" she asks you. What should you say and do?

8. Ross Easterfield wants you to prepare a model lease for his rental properties. He wants you to include in the lease a clause that waives "all warranties, express or implied, including the warranty of habitability." You know that the Supreme Court has ruled that the warranty of habitability is not waivable and have so informed Easterfield. He tells you, "Put it in anyway. Most of them won't know that and it will save us a dozen legal fees a year."

     What should you say and do?

9. Assume that you have been working hard for the past three months to try to get one of Ross Easterfield's properties rezoned for light industrial use. A warehouse once stood on the property, but the warehouse burned down six months ago in a fire that you always assumed was accidental.

     An employee with whom Ross has had a falling out has come to your office to tell you "what a reptile you are working for." In particular, she tells you that Easterfield paid her ten thousand dollars to set the fire that burned down the warehouse. "For him it was just a business proposition: He had a deal for a factory for the property and he didn't want to pay demolition costs." No one was hurt in the fire. The insurance company paid benefits without raising any questions.

     The rezoning process should not involve appearance before any tribunals and requires no representations on your part about the cause of the fire. May you continue your efforts on Easterfield's behalf?

PROBLEM SET B.
PRESENTATION OF TESTIMONY

1.   You are Jesse's attorney. During your third interview she tells you the following story about what happened on the night before she left the Easterfields'. She was in her room when the Easterfields returned home from the opera. After they went to their room, she went down to the library to get a book so that she could read herself to sleep. She saw Kerry Easterfield's brooch lying on the bookshelf where Kelly eventually found it. In a foolish moment, she took the brooch and brought it upstairs to her room. She had it there with her for about fifteen minutes when she realized what a foolish thing things she was doing. She brought it back downstairs and replaced it on the shelf.

   You are planning Jesse's direct examination. How will you deal with the above episode in the direct?

2.   You are Jesse's attorney. Before her deposition, she tells you the following story for the first time. She was awake when the Easterfields came home on the 16th. After they went to bed, she came downstairs to the library to get a book from the library. There on the table in the library was Kerry Easterfield's brooch. She thought about how beautiful the brooch was and how valuable it must be. She thought about how little the Easterfields paid her and about how rich they were. She took the brooch off the table and moved it to the shelf near the book with her name on it. She had not resolved to take the brooch, but wanted to be able to steal it if she decided to later. She returned to her room and there decided that it would be wrong to take the brooch. When Kerry asked her to find the brooch the next morning, Jesse became afraid and confused. She was afraid to go into the library and remove the brooch from where she had put it because she might be seen and someone might figure out what had happened. Foolish perhaps, but that is what she thought.

   You are preparing Jesse to testify. Discuss the above with her.

3.   Jesse tells you that she knew what Holman was going to do when he committed the robbery. She confides in you that she never told this to Reverend Taylor: "He has been so good to me and it would disappoint him so much." You decide to omit any reference to Jesse's "innocence" from her direct examination.

   Reverend Taylor remains convinced, based on his earlier conversations with Jesse and his review of the paper record, that Jesse was not guilty in the Holman matter. You want to call Taylor to give his expert opinion about the seriousness of the damages that Jesse suffered. In your preparation sessions, whenever you ask him why he thinks that Jesse was seriously injured by Ross's statements, he always says something like, "This was particularly destructive because it was the second time that Jesse had been falsely accused." He then tells the story about Jesse's incompetent and unethical lawyer.

   May you call Taylor as a witness and allow him to present this testimony? If not, what should you do?

Exercises & Problems in Professional Responsibility

4.   You are Joe's attorney. The day before trial, he tells you that he wants to testify that he was making love with Mrs. Porter from 9:45 until 10:30 in his room. She is now willing to corroborate this testimony. He didn't say anything about this at the first trial because Porter is involved with someone else whom she hopes to marry and this revelation would "ruin her life."

     (a) Assume that Joe and Porter are definite and unequivocal in their insistence that this is the truth.
     What should you do?

     (b) Assume that Joe and Porter are indefinite and contradict each other about the details of their tryst. Joe insists on testifying.
     You cannot convince him not to. What should you do?

5.   Assume that you are preparing Jesse to testify. Jesse tells you that Ross said to her in the library, "You stole my wife's brooch, you ungrateful little jailbird . . . " You have every reason to believe her. The problem is that at her deposition, she was asked this question and gave this answer:

Q.   At any time did Mr. Easterfield directly and verbally accuse you of stealing the brooch?

A.   No.

Jesse tells you, quite plausibly, that she didn't want to repeat at her deposition what Easterfield had said because it was so humiliating. She says, "I sort of just blanked out when they asked that question."
     Pick up the conversation with Jesse at that point.

PROBLEM SET C.
DISTRIBUTION OF AUTHORITY

1.   Joe is discussing the future trial with you. He tells you that he wants the case tried as a "referendum on the rights of men in our society." As part of that strategy, he wants you to introduce evidence of the death of his first wife so he can explain how the police unfairly and groundlessly accused him even though there was no evidence of his guilt.

You think the "strategy" unwise and likely to lead to his conviction. He is insistent and trial is in two weeks.

Discuss the matter with him. Explain to him what you will do.

2.   Ross Easterfield believes that you should try the case on the theory that Jesse tried to steal the brooch. What weight will you give his belief?

What if he tells you, "I don't give a good goddamn whether she took it or not. But we can sure as hell make her squirm and, who knows, if we win, maybe I'll be able to convince the prosecutor to bring charges. That means more to me than some marginal improvement in our chances of winning."

Discuss the matter with him.

3.   Your firm represents Jesse. The partner in charge of the case has told you that he wants to include a count for reckless infliction of emotional harm. He tells you he discussed it with Jesse and she said she wants that in the complaint. You researched the issue and found a case decided by the Nita Supreme Court four years ago which held that Nita does not recognize this tort. At the time of the Supreme Court decision all other states save four recognized it. Since the Nita Supreme Court decision, one other state has established the tort.

What should you do?

4.   Jesse tells you on the morning of trial that she wants you to strike all men and all blacks from the jury because she thinks that they will be unsympathetic to her cause. You know that "race-based peremptories" and "gender based peremptories" are forbidden under *Batson* and its progeny. You also know that sometimes a lawyer can convince a judge that he or she is exercising a strike for fabricated reasons, while successfully obscuring the true, race-or-gender-based motivation.

What should you do?

5.   Jesse has moved to a neighboring state. She says she wants to file her suit against Ross Easterfield in federal court because she "wants to make a federal case out of this." You believe that you have a slightly better chance in state court since the jury pool is a bit more working-class. On the other hand, it will take five years to get to trial in state court and "only" three in federal court. Jesse is insistent.

Must you file in federal court?

Exercises & Problems in Professional Responsibility

6.   Joe is convicted.
Must you represent him on appeal? Must you file the Notice of Appeal?

7.   Assume that Joe Mitchell is a juvenile. He is charged with murder in juvenile court and the prosecutor immediately files a motion that Joe be tried as an adult in the criminal courts.
Can you condition your representation of Joe on the case's remaining in juvenile court?

8.   You represent Ross Easterfield. You obtained a verdict for the defendant in the trial court. In the course of that victory, the trial judge made a number of indefensible evidentiary rulings, all of which favored your client. The plaintiff filed a timely Notice of Appeal, but then failed to file a document called the "abstract of record," in a timely way. That failure does not rob the appellate court of jurisdiction, but you know that the appellate court will almost always dismiss the appeal for want of prosecution upon the appellee's motion.
A second-year associate at the firm that represents Jesse, came to see you three days after the abstract was due. She told you that two days before the abstract was due, both her parents were killed in a house fire that the police believe was deliberately set. She was so upset and disoriented that she failed to mention the abstract to the partner at her firm when they inquired as to what had to be done in her absence. She asks you not to file the motion to dismiss the appeal. She says that it will end her career.
What should you do?

9.   You represent Ross Easterfield. He told you that he wants you to fight every continuance and motion for an extension of time. He says that he can't stand to have "this ridiculous suit" hanging over his head one day more than he has to.
What do you say? What should you do?

10.   You represent Ross Easterfield. You know that Jesse MacIntyre's lawyer is a solo practitioner who has taken the case on a contingency fee basis. You believe that this is potentially the biggest case she has and that she must "pay the bills" by taking a large number of smaller cases during the five years that this case will be pending. (You can probably stretch out the time to trial to seven years without raising the judge's ire and, more importantly, you can plausibly threaten to.)
You know that Jesse's lawyer is not above taking into consideration her own interests in representing an unsophisticated client.
May you take advantage of Jesse's lawyer's "cash flow" situation to achieve a more favorable settlement? Must you, ethically? Can you avoid doing so? Must you discuss this matter with your client?

11.   Assume Joe Mitchell is sixteen and is being tried as an adult for the murder of his girlfriend. The state has offered a plea to voluntary manslaughter, which carries a maximum penalty of eight years. Joe will have to serve only four at most, and there is a chance the judge will not impose the maximum. If he goes to trial and loses, he faces the death penalty and, failing that, natural life imprisonment.

He told you in confidence that he really did kill his girlfriend. You beg him to take the plea. He refuses. You believe that he simply does not understand his situation. You will not be able to call him as a witness because of what he has told you, and he would, in any event, make a terrible witness. He bears a strong resemblance to the late Sid Vicious. Because of extremely strict standards, he will not be found incompetent to stand trial, but he is so distracted that he is hardly able to help in his own defense.

What should you do?

12.   Assume that Jesse MacIntyre is seventeen years old, a year shy of the age at which she may vote and make binding contracts, but lucid and of average intelligence. Her legal guardian is Sister Rosetta Maria of the Divine Word orphanage in Nita City, where Jesse was brought up.

Sister Rosetta tells you that she wants you to dismiss the lawsuit against Easterfield. She tells you that Ross is a decent man who did right by Jesse and that Jesse is being ungrateful to him. Sister Rosetta also is angry at you for bringing the suit without her permission, and promises to bring a disciplinary action against you if you do not comply with the wishes of "Jesse's legal guardian."

Now assume that Sister Rosetta is, on her own motion, appointed guardian ad litem for the case. The day after she is appointed she tells you to settle the case for $20,000 , to be paid equally to Jesse and to the orphanage (for Jesse's past support).

What should you do?

13.   You believe that the sixteen-year-old Joe Mitchell is incompetent to stand trial. He has so "blocked" the incidents of the night of his girlfriend's killing that he literally cannot help you reconstruct the sequence of events and certainly cannot effectively testify to what occurred. This memory loss is consistent with the psychotic functioning that often accompanies borderline personality disorder when someone with that disorder is under great stress.

If he is found incompetent to stand trial, he will be placed in a state mental hospital for a year. If he is not competent to stand trial after a year, the criminal court will conduct a "discharge hearing" to determine if there exists evidence beyond a reasonable doubt of his guilt. If there is not, he will be released. If there is, he could be committed to state mental hospitals until he is competent (at which time he would stand trial) or the maximum length of the sentence he could receive, whichever is shorter. The maximum sentence for murder is natural life. Thus, he could easily spend the rest of his life in state mental hospitals. He prefers prison. He directs you not to assert that he is incompetent to stand trial. You think he is incompetent.

What should you do?

14. Ross Easterfield's counsel fails to object to evidence of apparently privileged conversations between Ross and Kerry Easterfield. On appeal, Ross's appellate counsel urges that Easterfield explicitly told his counsel to assert the privilege at trial and that the lawyer simply failed to do so. Ross claims that since he had not authorized his lawyer's action, it ought not to be imputed to him.
      Result?

15. Ross Easterfield's counsel signs a document settling the pending lawsuit for $500,000. An agreed judgment for that amount is entered. Three weeks later, Easterfield's new counsel files a motion to vacate the judgment, supported by Ross's affidavit that he was unaware of his former counsel's action in settling the case and that he never authorized settling the case for more than $200,000.
      Should the judge schedule an evidentiary hearing or simply deny the motion on the ground that the lawyer was acting as the client's agent with apparent authority on which the plaintiff was entitled to rely?

16. Joe Mitchell's lawyer has too much to drink one afternoon and starts to tell the local bartender about how tough it is to be a lawyer. He tells the bartender about having to defend "a guy who has killed two wives in a row." Joe's lawyer complains to the bartender, "The guy looks me right in the eye and says, 'Yeah, I killed both of them, and don't regret it one bit.'" The prosecution calls the bartender, arguing that Joe's lawyer has waived the privilege.
      Result?

17. What if it was Jesse MacIntyre's lawyer who told the bartender that Jesse said that she did, in fact, try to steal the brooch.
      Could the defense call the bartender? What if Jesse had testified in court that she had not tried to steal the brooch and the bartender was called in rebuttal?

18. Can you state in general terms the rule that explains the results in Problems 14–17?

19. Jesse MacIntyre's lawyers are concerned that she will foolishly settle the case for merely reinstatement or some kind of apology, after her lawyers put in hundreds of hours work in preparing the case. They expect to represent her for a contingency fee.
      Can they put a clause in their retainer agreement allowing them to prevent a settlement of which they do not approve? Can they ask for a nonrefundable retainer? If not, how might they "protect themselves"? *Should* they take those steps?

20.   Ross Easterfield proposes to offer the testimony of a lawyer from the firm that is trying the *MacIntyre* case for him. The prospective witness does exclusively management-side labor law. Ross wants to present testimony that the day after Jesse left the house, he called his lawyer and asked what he should say about her if he received inquiries from prospective employers. The lawyer would testify that she told Easterfield that it was his duty to answer all inquiries with complete candor, and explicitly told Easterfield that any prospective employer was entitled to the benefit of an honest opinion about Jesse's honesty. Furthermore, the lawyer told Easterfield that Ross would be liable to any prospective employer for any lack of full candor.

What issues are implicated in Ross's offer of proof?

Exercises & Problems in Professional Responsibility

PROBLEM SET D.
INVESTIGATION, DISCOVERY, AND CONTACTS WITH WITNESSES

1.   You represent Ross Easterfield. You receive a telephone call from the cook at the Easterfield home. He tells you that he thought it was "a shame the way they drove Jesse away." He then offers to keep you apprised of developments around the Easterfield home, especially the relationship between Mr. and Mrs. Easterfield.

   May you accept his offer? May you ask him to keep a written record of every time that Mrs. Easterfield misplaces a piece of jewelry? If it is ethically permissible, and it is tactically advantageous, is it ethically obligatory? Are there any purely tactical reasons why you may be reluctant to accept the offer?

2.   You represent Jesse MacIntyre. You receive a call from the wife of the investigator for the firm that represents Easterfield. She tells you that she is upset that her husband, for whom she seems to have little respect, is working on the Easterfields' behalf. She thinks that Easterfield's case is a "real stinker." She says that her husband "talks a blue streak" about his work and asks you if it would help Jesse if she just "passes along" what she learns.

   What do you say?

3.   You represent Joe Mitchell. You stop at the Silver Dollar Saloon for a beer after work. The bartender starts speaking about the "weirdos" she has met in the course of her job. She mentions your client, whom she knows was charged with killing his wife soon after leaving the bar. The bartender appears to be hostile to your client; perhaps the sort of potential witness who would choose not to speak with defense counsel. Without any encouragement from you, she launches into a long description of how Joe appeared on the night of the killing.

   May you simply sit and listen? Ask an occasional encouraging question to keep her going?

4.   You represent Jesse MacIntyre. You made a Freedom of Information request to the state Bureau of Occupational Licensing, whose records are fully covered under the Freedom of Information Act, seeking Ross Easterfield's application for a real estate license and the record of complaints against him. Apparently at Easterfield's urging, the attorney general of the State of Nita, subsequently filed a disciplinary complaint against you for making the request directly to the licensing bureau. The attorney general alleges that she, the attorney general, represents the bureau and that your request was in violation of Rule 4.2.

   Do you have anything to worry about?

5.   Jesse MacIntyre comes to see you for the first time. No lawsuit has been filed. She tells you about her dealings with Ross Easterfield and says that what she really wants is a reconciliation with him. She says that she wants to avoid "all this lawyer stuff." On the other hand, she says that if he won't "listen to my side" she is prepared to sue. You suspect that Easterfield has a general practitioner as a family lawyer and often employs a real estate law firm for his business dealings. In all probability, he is unaware of a possible slander lawsuit and has not engaged counsel for the case that MacIntyre

Exercises & Problems in Professional Responsibility

is contemplating.

How should you proceed to communicate MacIntyre's perspective to Easterfield?

6. You represent Ross Easterfield. Your client told you about an ongoing criminal investigation of the finances at the club. In particular, the United States Attorney is interested in a deduction Easterfield took for a $50,000 contribution to the club's charitable foundation. The club seems to be missing about $40,000 and the U.S. Attorney suspects that the money was channeled back to Easterfield. Tax fraud is suspected: the club keeps $10,000 and Ross gets a $50,000 tax deduction. Only the federal treasury loses. You have concluded that Easterfield's interests are best served by remaining silent and invoking the Fifth Amendment whenever necessary.

Marlow comes to your office and asks your advice on this matter. You believe that Marlow's testimony could hurt Easterfield and you advise her not to say anything to the prosecution unless she is subpoenaed. You tell Marlow this because she has some small exposure herself and if she voluntarily came forward the prosecutor might consider an offer of immunity.

May you advise Marlow to keep silent unless she is subpoenaed?

7. You represent Jesse MacIntyre and you expect trial to begin in two weeks. Kelly Emerson calls and tells you that her lease is up tomorrow and she intends to return to her childhood home in a distant state, where a job awaits her. She says that as a favor to Jesse she will stay in the jurisdiction if you pay her hotel bills for two weeks (or get Reverend Taylor to put her up at the St. James Home). She also wants you to pay her what she would have made if she had started her new job two weeks earlier, about $900.

8. You represent Ross Easterfield. You are discussing discovery strategy with your private investigator, who is an independent contractor with your firm. You explain that in your opinion, Jesse is holding back in her job searches in order to build up her damages. Your investigator tells you of some friends who own small businesses who owe the investigator favors. She suggests that they contact Jesse and offer her positions that "involve some real work" at salaries higher than what she is receiving at St. James. If Jesse refuses, then they could testify to her failure to mitigate damages. The investigator suggests that this testimony may even have an effect on the liability portion of the trial: The jury may conclude that Jesse is a manipulative person who doesn't deserve an award.

What do you say to your investigator's offer? In housing discrimination cases, "testers" of different races routinely pretend to be interested in renting or buying in order to gather evidence of discrimination. Is what your investigator proposes any different from what "testers" do in housing discrimination cases?

9. You represent Jesse MacIntyre. You are considering hiring an expert who can testify about the effects of Ross's actions on Jesse's psychological state and her job prospects. You have contacted Dr. Fiona Coughlin who teaches occupational psychology at Yale. She sent along a brochure that describes her credentials and fee schedule. Her credentials are strong and her fee schedule looks

attractive. She charges $3,000 to do an initial review of the papers in the case. As part of that same price, she sends a detailed opinion letter. If, based on the opinion letter, you decide not to use her as your testifying expert in the case, she will refund $1,500 of the initial fee. If you do decide to use Dr. Coughlin as your testifying expert, her fee is $200 per hour.

May you retain her under this arrangement?

10.   You represent Ross Easterfield. You are thinking about the damages aspect of the case. You don't yet know who the plaintiff will designate as her testifying expert on the psychological effects of Easterfield's actions and their effects on Jesse' job prospects. It may be Reverend Taylor, whose credentials you regard as weak. You really fear that the plaintiff will engage Dr. Peter Franz, who teaches occupational psychology at Nita University. Franz has written an authoritative text in the field and you know him to be a very engaging speaker and an excellent witness.

You don't expect to call your own expert in this field. You really want to keep the plaintiff from calling Franz, however, and you regard it "worth a couple thousand" to engage Franz yourself as a "consulting expert," so as to keep the plaintiff from calling him. (You know that the ethics of his own profession would not allow him to work on both sides of the same case.) You expect that Franz may be of some help in preparing to cross-examine Taylor, but if you faced the question honestly you would have to say that you would not hire him for that purpose if there were no danger of his testifying for the plaintiff.

May you engage Franz as a consulting expert? You know, by the way, that you would likely pay Franz about two thousand dollars for his efforts, while he would likely earn upwards of ten thousand if he testified for the plaintiff.

Is it good enough that you have a "good faith" reason to employ Franz, one that you could plausibly advance if challenged? Is your opponent entitled to the benefit of a more refined analysis of your own motives?

11.   You are an associate in the law firm that represents Ross Easterfield. Discovery has not yet begun, but the case has been placed on the local "rocket docket," and you expect to try the case in about six months. The partner who is in charge of the case tells you that Easterfield has convinced the club's board of directors to support an internship for Marlow in three world-class European spas which will take her abroad for nine months. The partner smiles and says, "Ross is no fool. MacIntyre's lawyers are unlikely to front the money to fly to Provence for a deposition in this kind of case! And maybe Ross does want Marlow to bring a little continental ambience to Nita City. Let's stay out of this one."

What do you say? Can you safely rely on the partner's judgment?

12.   The same partner wants you to get a list of all the current and past domestic workers at the Easterfields' home, and a list of all the employees and ex-employees of the club over the past three years and call them up. The partner wants you to tell them "something like" the following: "You won't be helping Mr. Easterfield or the club if you talk to MacIntyre's lawyers. You should know that if you

say something that they like, you may have to miss several days of work in order to testify. That will come out of your pocket, except for a measly witness fee."

He wants you to get a definite commitment from each of them at least not to talk with MacIntyre's lawyers until someone from your office can arrive.

If you feel uncomfortable doing these things, can you suggest that one of the firm's investigators make the calls?

13.   You represent Ross Easterfield. You receive a call from the ABC Employment Agency. Winsor tells you that she has a little confession to make. She says that in order to "protect ourselves," the agency has been routinely taping interviews with the references that their clients provide. No one knows about these tapes, and the agency, just as routinely, destroys them after keeping them for a year. It is now the month in which the agency received the call from Easterfield, and the agency would erase that tape in due course, this afternoon.

You are deeply concerned about what that tape may contain. In your gut, you believe it is probably bad for your case.

Winsor asks you what to do. How should you respond?

14.   You represent Easterfield. The partner in charge of the case calls you into her office and tells you that she has just returned from a mandatory CLE legal ethics seminar, in which they discussed Rule 4.2, and says she has a "bright idea." She says she wants you to call each of the current and former employees at the club and offer to represent them in any role they might have as a witness in the *MacIntyre* case. You can explain to the employees that, "MacIntyre's lawyers will then have to contact me (rather than the employee) and I can keep them from bothering you." The partner smiles and says, "See, legal ethics can have some uses."

How should you respond?

15.   You represent Jesse MacIntyre. Your investigator brings you a number of dog-eared documents that you are pleased to see. They are memos from Marlow to the "Applicant's File." Though the documents are crumpled and half illegible, you can make out what they are. They contain close to verbatim notes on interviews that Marlow has had with applicants for work at the club, including boxes checked either "Make Offer" or "No Offer." They cover the month before Marlow's interview with Jesse. You have to wonder whether such a document exists for Marlow's interview with Jesse, and you have to wonder whether it will still exist at the time of Marlow's deposition next month.

You ask your investigator where she got the file. She says that about an hour before the usual pick-up, she just picked up the garbage that was put out by the administrative office of the club. It was out in the alley, he protests. There was no need to enter onto private property.

The investigator says, "You call the shots, my friend. The next pick-up is tomorrow at 7:00." What do you say?

What else might you do?

16.   You are an associate in the law firm that represents Ross Easterfield. The partner in charge of the case knows that your father's best friend is department chief of the Nita Department of Occupational Licensing. That department administers real estate licenses in Nita City. The partner tells you that he wants to be able to tell Easterfield that no one from the department will, without subpoena, testify about Easterfield's reputation for truthfulness in the "regulatory community."

The partner asks, "Could you try to get an informal commitment from your dad's friend so I can reassure Ross?"

How should you respond?

17.   Your firm represents Ross Easterfield's real estate company, Xerxes Realty, Inc. You are about to file a lawsuit against the Jones Electric, Inc. for electrical work they did in an apartment complex Xerxes was developing. Faulty wiring in the main circuit box caused a fire that destroyed the almost-completed complex.

The partner in charge of the suit wants you to go alone, before the case is filed, to interview the electrician who wired the box. He also wants you to interview the two Jones Electric Company laborers who were apparently the first persons to see the fire.

May you conduct the interviews?

18.   While interviewing the latter two people, one of them says, "Let me tell you exactly what I told Jones's lawyers."

May you respond, "Well, please do"?

19.   You find out that one of the two laborers was in charge of site security, including fire prevention, and that after the fire he gave a long oral description of the work done on the main circuit box to his boss.

May you ask him what he told his boss?

20.   The partner on the case thinks that Jones's attorneys will probably want to interview the inspectors from Xerxes who had examined the box on the morning of the fire. She tells you to draft a memo from Easterfield to all Xerxes corporate employees, instructing them not to discuss the fire with any attorneys for Jones Electric and to urge Ross to circulate it. He also tells you to tell Easterfield to call all the other subcontractors and order them not to allow their employees to discuss the fire with Jones' attorneys.

Should you do what your partner asks?

PROBLEM SET E.
NEGOTIATION

1.   You represent Ross Easterfield, who is anxious to settle this case. You have in mind a structured settlement that would pay Jesse MacIntyre $25,000 per year for the next five years. You honestly believe that such a settlement may be in Jesse's best interests. Ross tells you that he is "cash-starved" right now, but expects some major deals to pay off within the next couple years, and so would prefer to pay more later, rather than less now.

You are concerned that Jesse's lawyers strongly prefer a "big hit" now in order to enhance their immediate contingency fee. They have verbally dismissed your inquiries about a structured settlement and you believe that they have not discussed it with their client. You are preparing a letter to Jesse's lawyers setting out the terms of a structured settlement.

May you send a copy to Jesse, just to make sure that she is aware of the offer? How about sending one to Reverend Taylor?

2.   You represent Jesse MacIntyre. In the give-and-take of negotiating a settlement, Easterfield's lawyers ask, "Does MacIntyre want to file an employment discrimination action against Easterfield?" You answer, "She's seriously considering it." In fact, you have no reason to believe that she has ever thought of doing that. After the negotiation, you realize that in the heat of things you have distorted the truth.

What should you do? What if your answer had been, "She hasn't ruled it out"?

3.   Assume that Jesse MacIntyre sued both Mr. and Mrs. Easterfield for slander. Assume further, that Mrs. Easterfield filed for divorce and moved out of the Easterfield home. It is clear to you that Mr. Easterfield is the more culpable of the two and has the "deep pocket."

May you offer to drop Mrs. Easterfield from the suit in return for her cooperating with you in presenting your case? You tell her that of course you want her to tell only the truth, but you ask that she come to your office so that you may prepare her to testify in the trial against her ex-husband.

4.   You represent Jesse MacIntyre and are on the verge of settling with Easterfield when you receive the sad news of Jesse's death in an automobile accident. Jesse has a sister, Nora, who is her sole heir and for whom Jesse had a lot of affection. Nora is quite poor herself. Ross's lawyer calls and says he wants to meet with you tomorrow to settle the case, claiming to have a cashier's check for $150,000.

What should you do?

5.   It is the day of trial and you represent Ross. Three weeks ago, you made your final offer of $100,000 in an oral conversation with Jesse's lawyers. They refused the offer the next day. You meet Kelly Emerson in the hall and say, "Hello." She stops for a chat and tells you that what has really made Jesse angry is the fact that Easterfield has made no offers to settle during the past year.

What should you do?

Exercises & Problems in Professional Responsibility

6.   You are representing Jesse MacIntyre in settlement negotiations with Easterfield. During your initial interviews with Jesse, she told you that she had one conversation with Easterfield a month after leaving his house and before coming to see you. During that conversation, she told Easterfield that she had been turned down by thirty potential employers since leaving his house and had voluntarily committed herself to a mental hospital for ten days. Neither of these things was true, she tells you, but she just wanted "him to feel as bad as I did."

During the negotiations, your opponent mentions to you that she supposed that Jesse's "mental breakdown" and "many disappointments" in seeking employment are "worth something." She then made an offer of $200,000 to settle the case. What should you do?

PROBLEM SET F.
FEES AND CLIENT PROPERTY

1.   The Model Rules prohibit or limit certain arrangements that contain inherent conflicts between lawyer and client. *See e.g.,* Rule 1.8(c), (d), and (h). Consider the contingency fee arrangement between Jesse MacIntyre and her lawyers in Exercise 7.

Doesn't such an agreement inevitably pose deep conflicts between lawyer and client, at least as severe as the prohibited conflicts? Would an hourly fee arrangement remove any conflict?

2.   Assume that MacIntyre's attorneys become aware in the first interview that she may prefer a nonmonetary settlement with Easterfield. They are concerned that such a settlement would render their usual contingency fee contract worthless.

How could they ethically protect their financial interests? By insisting on a "veto" of any settlement agreement? Otherwise? *Should* they protect themselves?

3.   Jesse MacIntyre has retained "Big Hit Harry" Holderman. He charges a 55 percent contingency fee, regardless of when the case ends, whether before filing or after appeal. He has developed a specialty in obtaining punitive damages, many times the amount of the "actual" damages. Insurance companies do tend to settle when he calls. Assume he settles the case for $100,000 after interviewing Jesse and meeting with Ross Easterfield's insurance lawyers, a total of twelve hours work.

Is his fee "reasonable"?

4.   Ross Easterfield interviews a small litigation firm, which tells him that they will consider representing him in his defamation action. Two days after the interview, he receives the following letter concerning fees:

Dear Mr. Easterfield:

When you interviewed with us last week, we told you that a letter would follow detailing the fee arrangement under which we would accept your case. We are indeed willing to represent you under the following conditions.

You will be billed on an hourly basis. The hourly rate will be determined by the novelty and difficulty of the questions that your case presents, and the skill that the resolution of those questions requires. There is no way to determine in advance what the precise hourly rate, as determined by those factors, will be. Unanticipated and difficult jurisdictional, procedural, and evidentiary issues may arise in the course of a suit, which simply cannot be predicted at the outset. Nor, can we be sure of the time and labor that their competent resolution will require.

The fact that Ms. MacIntyre is suing you for $1 million dictates that substantial time and effort in defense are warranted. Our firm will have to forego other opportunities to clear adequate time for the competent handling of this case and specific deadlines for discovery and

Exercises & Problems in Professional Responsibility

the answering of plaintiff motions, for example with regard to discovery, may require periods of intense work. Our firm, as you know, was recently described in the *Nita Lawyer* magazine as one of the six "coming" small litigation firms in Nita.

We will bill you on a monthly basis. Retaining us will authorize all expenditure of attorney time that we, in our professional judgment, believe appropriate in the course of any month.

Sincerely,

H. Priscilla Black
Managing Partner

Does the letter set forth an ethically permissible fee arrangement?

5.   Joe Mitchell is paying his lawyers on an hourly basis.
      May his lawyers go to Indianapolis to interview Kiley without seeking his permission? The time and costs of the trip will be approximately $2,800.

6.   Ross Easterfield pays a sum of $50,000 to his lawyers, which the written fee arrangement refers to as a "nonrefundable retainer." The fee arrangement provides for an hourly rate of $250 to be charged against that retainer until it is depleted, whereupon Easterfield will pay additional $20,000 advances against which further fees will be charged.
      Must they deposit the advance in a client trust fund until the money is earned? The case settles after Easterfield's lawyers have spent seven hours on the matter. May his lawyers keep the entire $50,000 retainer? What if it had been a $5,000 retainer?

7.   Ross Easterfield's lawyers propose to take one-tenth interest in the Bloomsbury Gardens development as the fee for defending him in the defamation action. The offer is attractive to Ross.
      May the bargain be struck on those terms?

8.   Joe Mitchell's lawyer contracts to provide his defense for $35,000, but the contract provides that the lawyer will withdraw if Joe is convicted because counsel does not want to do the mitigation hearing in a potential death penalty case.
      Permissible? *could be OK, negotiate terms of contract*

9.   Jesse MacIntyre's lawyers propose to represent her "only to achieve a settlement" in the case. They propose to take a 25 percent contingency fee and to withdraw if they cannot settle at least a month before the trial date.
      Permissible?

10.   George does tax law for small businesses and individuals. Jesse walks into his office. He calls Jane, who is a trial specialist. He believes that Jane is the most decent person and best trial lawyer he knows. He tells Jane that he has a prospect and will send her over if they agree to split the contingent fee that Jane will charge. Jane says the usual fee is 30 percent, but that she will charge 40 percent if she has to split it. George agrees, and agrees, too, that he will be jointly responsible for any malpractice Jane commits. George explains frankly that he intends to do no work on the case after the referral, except to look at the settlement for possible tax consequences, something that should take fifteen minutes.
      Permissible? *not permissible b/c no benefit to the client*

11.   Assume that Jesse will also bring an employment discrimination claim against Ross. The cause of action provides for statutory fees, based on the hourly rate of plaintiff's counsel. You told Jesse when you took the case that you would "seek fees against Easterfield if we prevail" and "you won't have to pay anything." Easterfield offers to settle the case for $50,000 to Jesse and no fees to you.
      Advise Jesse whether she should accept the settlement.

12.   Reverend Taylor agrees to pay an hourly fee for your firm to represent Jesse MacIntyre in her defamation action. He tells you that he really believes that Jesse is much too eager to accept reinstatement and has agreed with Jesse that, in return for his paying her fees, your firm will take its direction on the terms of settlement from him.
      May you represent Jesse under these conditions?

13.   Your contingency fee agreement with Jesse MacIntyre provides for a fee of "33 percent of the recovery, plus litigation costs." The recovery is $90,000 and the costs are $15,000.
      (a) How much do you receive?
      (b) May your fee agreement provide that Jesse is responsible for litigation costs only in the event of a recovery adequate to cover them?

14.   You were successful in winning a $10 million award against Ross Easterfield. A number of journalists wrote essays in the "it's about time this guy got whacked" vein. One approached you with interest in writing a long essay in a local magazine about "the waif and the real estate wizard." She offers you one-half of the $20,000 fee for sitting down with her for about four hours.
      May you do it?

15.   Jesse MacIntyre has sued for $1 million. Ross Easterfield's lawyer drafts a contingency fee contract under which they will received as a fee 10 percent of the difference between $1 million and the amount actually awarded.
      Should the court enforce the award? Why or why not?

16.   Joe is acquitted and Brooke is charged with murder. She wants to enter into a fee agreement under which she will pay her lawyers $35,000 out of the proceeds of the life insurance policy she has on Leslie. She may not recover on the policy if a "criminal court of competent jurisdiction adjudicates the beneficiary to have committed any degree of criminal homicide against the insured."
      May you represent Brooke under those conditions?

17.   Mr. and Mrs. Easterfield have divorced. After the divorce decree was entered, Mrs. Easterfield came to believe that Ross had hidden certain resources during the divorce proceedings. She entered into a contingency fee agreement for 20 percent of the value of any new property that her new lawyer might cause to be divided.
      May a lawyer enter into such an agreement?

18.   Ross Easterfield pays you a $20,000 retainer against which your fee of $200 per hour will be drawn. Your senior partner tells you to deposit the $20,000 in the firm's general account.
      Should you?

19.   Ross also pays you $5,000 for costs of filing fees and deposition fees. Your partner tells you to deposit this money in a "litigation fund" in which all such client advance payments are mingled and from which checks are written. The partner tells you to be sure to note the deposit on the office's own internal computerized ledger system, credited to Easterfield's account, from which debits are also noted.
      Permissible?

20.   You represent Jesse MacIntyre. You have just received a settlement check for $80,000 made out to both Jesse and yourself. Unfortunately Jesse and you have had a disagreement about the interpretation of your fee agreement. She maintains that you are entitled to $25,000 in fees and you believe that you are entitled to $35,000. Your jurisdiction recognizes an attorney's charging liens on judgments.
      What should you do with the check?

21. A lawyer at your firm represented Jesse pursuant to a 40 percent contingency fee agreement. He withdrew from further representation after working on her case for 200 hours. He withdrew, because Jesse refused to agree with the lawyer's advice that she accept only settlements of over $50,000. With new counsel, Jesse then accepted a settlement for $100,000. You sit on the management committee of your firm and Jesse's former lawyer wants the firm to sue her on a *quantum meruit* theory.

Should you?

Exercises & Problems in Professional Responsibility

PROBLEM SET G.
CROSS-EXAMINATION

1.   During your fourth interview with Joe Mitchell, he broke down in tears and admitted killing his wife while trying to shoot his mother-in-law. He told you to explore the possibility of a plea bargain, but the state would agree only to an "open plea," that is, a plea where the court was committed in advance to no specific sentence. The state would promise only that they would present the evidence "in aggravation" but would not affirmatively argue for the death penalty. Following your advice, Joe declined the offer. You had no choice but to go to trial.

For obvious reasons, Joe will not testify at his trial. Your theory of the case is mistaken identity. In opening statement, you told a story of Joe's actions on the night of the killing that was consistent with his testimony at his first trial. You knew to a moral certainty that what you were telling the jury was false.

In so doing, did you violate your professional responsibilities? Would it have been better for you to waive opening and simply test the state's evidence on cross-examination?

Or perhaps, rather than giving an affirmative (and false) account, you should have only said that the state's evidence will not show beyond a reasonable doubt that Joe was the killer, then you could have said some general things, urging the jury to keep an open mind until the entire case is over.

If you viewed either of these latter as even slightly tactically inferior, might you consider doing them because they are ethically preferable? Should you at least have asked Joe whether you could do either of them?

2.   Assume Joe told you something more. He said that he is not a mystery novelist for nothing. As part of his plan he slipped into the Wilson home at 9 P.M. and set the clock on the mantel ahead by fifteen minutes. When Brooke heard it ringing 10 o'clock, it was really 9:45. In fact, he went from the Ravenna gun shop at 9:40, shot Leslie at 9:45, and arrived back at Porter's at 9:55. He counted on no one noticing that the clock was wrong, and in fact, no one did.

During your cross may you dwell on the fact that the clock was ringing 10:00, asking many inconsequential questions just to emphasize the time? ("Now you are quite sure that it was not ringing 9 o'clock? I know this is difficult for you, but it is very important. The clock started ringing just as Leslie rang the doorbell? Might it have been a few seconds before? But not more than a few seconds?")

What if Joe told you that he had set the clock ahead earlier that day with the intent to kill Brooke but repented of it as the day wore on? Assume he really convinces you that he did not do the killing. Should you do anything differently?

3.   Would your cross-examination of Brooke Thompson on her visit to the foundry be any different if her statement read as follows: "Yes, I did go to the foundry just to see what was going on there and to look at the vats of liquid metal, but I certainly did not throw anything into any of the vats."

PROBLEM SET H.
IN-COURT BEHAVIOR

1.   You are standing in front of the judge during Joe Mitchell's bail hearing. You have argued that Joe is not a risk of flight and that he ought to receive bail of $50,000 ($5,000 "to walk"). The prosecutor has emphasized the seriousness of the crime and asked that Mitchell not be granted bail. The judge shuffles through a small pile of papers and says, "Well, since the defendant has not so much as an arrest on his record, I'm inclined to set bond as the defense suggests." The prosecutor shuffles through her papers and says nothing.

Joe told you that he was arrested briefly in connection with his first wife's death and was arrested and prosecuted (though not convicted) in the assault of another woman.

The judge asks you, "Anything else?"

What do you say?

2.   You are an associate in the law firm that will represent Ross Easterfield in the upcoming lawsuit. The firm's most well-known, some would say notorious, trial lawyer will first-chair the case. You have been assigned to second chair. These are the instructions the first chair gives you:

A. "Wear a dark brown suit early in the trial. As the trial progresses move to lighter shades of brown and finally to tan. Brown seems down-to-earth and sincere. All the studies show that. The progression to lighter shades symbolizes the lifting of a dark cloud of false accusation from the defendant. I think it works."

B. "Some of the jurors may hold it against Ross that he is childless. I want you to hire three young children to sit with Mrs. Easterfield throughout the trial. Call any one of the acting agencies; They always have a trainload of aspiring child actors. At breaks, Mr. Easterfield will walk over and talk to all of them and pick up the children in his arms. It should play."

C. "The jury box in this courtroom is positioned so that the sun sets in the jury's eyes. The clerk never notices it or she doesn't care. You can only get away with this once during the trial. Wait for a time after 3:30 P.M. when the plaintiff is really scoring some points and get up and start playing with the blinds so that eventually the sun isn't in the jurors' eyes any more. First, they'll be watching what you are doing rather than hearing the trial. And then they'll thank you for what you did. Perfect!"

3.   You are an assistant prosecutor second-chairing the case against Joe Mitchell. The lead prosecutor hands you a file which says in large letters written across the front, "VIOLENCE AGAINST WIVES: MURDER. CASE NUMBER 1005" In fact, this is the 1005th case in which a husband has been prosecuted for a violent crime against his wife this year in Nita City. Your boss tells you to place the file on the prosecutor's table so that the large letters are legible from the jury box. He has also organized the prosecution file in three portable file drawers. He tells you to stack the file drawers on the far side of your table so that the defense team cannot see half the jury during the trial.

What do you say and do?

Exercises & Problems in Professional Responsibility

4.   You are prosecuting Joe Mitchell. Mitchell is being represented by an eminent criminal defense attorney who has gained some notoriety (sometimes successfully) representing husbands accused of killing their wives. Your boss hands you a slip of paper and says, "I want you to do voir dire. Memorize this and slip it into your questioning of one of the jurors:

> Most of you have probably heard of Mr. Jones, who will be representing Joseph Mitchell here. Mr. Jones is probably *the* lawyer that a husband accused of shooting his wife wants to have. He is the best.
> You understand that in our system of justice, a defendant may hire any lawyer he can afford. Will anyone hold it against Joseph Mitchell that he has decided that he needs to hire probably the most eminent lawyer available to represent a husband who is accused of killing his wife?"

What should you do?

5.   You are prosecuting Mitchell in a state which imposes capital punishment by electric chair. You are seeking the death penalty.
      Your first chair tells you she wants you to make a little "bzzzzt" sound whenever you walk past Mitchell, making sure that the jury cannot hear you. She says, "It would be great if the jury were to see the kind of temper this guy really has!"
      Well?

6.   You are second-chairing the defense of Mitchell and are about to conduct the last pretrial preparation session with your client. The partner on the case tells you to be sure to remind Mitchell that you will have short chat with him before accepting jurors for the panel. He is to nod his head affirmatively after each such chat so that each juror chosen believes that Joe is personally approving his or her selection for the panel."
      What should you do?

7.   You work in a firm with a criminal defense department that has three partners and eight associates. One of the associates is a black woman, Susan Smith. The partner who will try the Mitchell case is a white man. He calls three associates, including the black woman, into his office two months before trial and says, "Peter and I can handle this trial. However, if there are more than two black persons on the jury, I want Susan involved." He turns to Smith and says, "I want you to prepare to do two direct examinations. If there are African-Americans on the jury, you are in. If not, you can spend your time better doing something else."

8.   Jesse MacIntyre asks you to represent a friend in a speeding case. Her friend, Kelly, will stand trial next week. Kelly tells you that when she was stopped she did not have her license with her and gave a false name, that of her sister. Reverend Taylor bailed her out without her ever having to

show her license. She did this for two reasons: (1) She has two previous speeding convictions and she would lose her license if convicted again, and (2) she is in this country illegally. Her sister is willing to go along. You know that the penalty for a first offense will be a $100 fine and that will be the end of it.

May you simply plea bargain the case?

9.   You are prosecuting Joe Mitchell. Your first chair tells you, "During your opening I want you to say, 'The evidence will show that Mitchell had been violent toward women under similar circumstances before.' I expect that we should be able to get in at least *one* of the earlier incidents. If we can't, we can at least tell the appellate court that we had a good-faith argument for their admissibility. And, as long as you don't get any more specific, any unfulfilled promise' should be viewed as harmless error. It's low risk and our job is to win trials, not worry too much about appeals."

What should you say?

PROBLEM SET I.
CONFIDENTIALITY

1.   Jesse had to visit several law firms before she could find one that would take her case. After she left the offices of the second attorney, she visited George Ryan, he called Easterfield, whom Ryan knew socially, and told Easterfield to "take preemptive action" to stop the suit that Jesse was planning.

    You learned of this conversation at Easterfield's deposition. When you called Ryan to verify what Easterfield had said, he openly admitted contacting Easterfield. "As soon as I learned that she wanted to sue Easterfield, I told her that I was a friend of his and that I would not represent her. I never had an attorney-client relation with her. Hell, I didn't even charge her for the consult. Anyway, since I wasn't her lawyer, I had no duties of confidentiality."

    Is Ryan right?

2.   You attended an alumni gathering at your law school the month after you began to represent Easterfield. (You are representing him only in the lawsuit brought by MacIntyre.) You found yourself chatting with a classmate who went into banking after law school and is now working at the Fidelity Loan Company. During a conversation about the relative merits of a career in banking and law practice, your classmate says:

> We have our share of jerks, of course. One guy in particular comes to mind, a wealthy realtor named Easterfield. Just yesterday, he comes roaring into my bank and starts yelling at me that he wants me to file a criminal complaint against this poor mope who made a minor mistake on a loan application. He tells me that she has stolen "a whole bunch of valuable things" and he wants "justice." Then the same guy removes all the money from the CDs that he and his wife own jointly, and moves the money to accounts that are in his name. Then he asks me if the bank works with a broker who can sell off his wife's jewelry without her knowing it. "She's got too damn much of it and I'll have the cash before she knows it's missing."

    May you inform Jesse of Easterfield's statement to the banker? May you inform Mrs. Easterfield of Mr. Easterfield's actions and proposed actions? Must you?

3.   You are Brooke Thompson's attorney. Sadly, Brooke stepped in front of the 5:10 train three weeks ago in what the police thought was a suicide committed in grief over her step-daughter's death. You know different. She had confessed to you that she had killed Leslie but that she could not bear the anxiety over being discovered. The state intends to proceed with Joe's prosecution.

    What should you do?

4.   Your firm has declined to represent Easterfield in his arson-for-profit schemes or in his Bloomsbury project. A month after you declined to represent him in either of these ventures, a man comes into your office and claims to be the brother of a man whom Easterfield has hired to burn down an abandoned warehouse in a remote location in Nita County, the next night. He tells you that he

can't come forward, but that he knows you represent Easterfield and wants you to tip-off the police. He says that there is no danger to life from any fires at the warehouse.

May you reveal what you know?

5.   You know of Easterfield's plans for the Bloomsbury project by reviewing documents he has provided you. All these plans have been filed with the Environmental Protection Agency and are subject to Freedom of Information requests. You know that Easterfield's plans for the Bloomsbury project will result in a tripling of the land values of adjacent parcels. You are considering purchasing the parcels.

(A) In order to take advantage of what you perceive to be an opportunity, you have to get financing to purchase those parcels, either through a bank or from individual investors. May you share what you know with them in order to buy the property?

(B) Assume that your law practice has been extremely successful and you do not need financing. May you simply start buying up the property? May you ask your client whether he has any objection and proceed if there is no objection?

Is the result different in either case if you are no longer representing Easterfield?

6.   While preparing Joe to testify, he tells you that he won the Congressional Medal of Honor while serving in Desert Storm. (He refused to abandon wounded buddies and held off a superior force until reinforcements arrived.) He tells you, however, that he does not want you to tell the prosecutor about this or to elicit it from him on the stand. He says that whole thing is "too sacred to use as a bargaining chip." You think that his being a war hero would significantly help him in plea bargaining or in front of the jury. Of course, it is a matter of public record.

May you mention it to the prosecutor? May you mention it in opening statement and then ask Joe about it on direct?

7.   You were Joe Mitchell's lawyer during his first trial. While you were investigating the case, you interviewed Mrs. Porter, who told you at first that she really wasn't sure about the time Joe arrived home on September 10. (She then recalled the time with more specificity.) Porter has testified in the second trial, and the prosecutor wants to impeach her with her initial statement of uncertainty to you, which she had earlier admitted to the prosecutor but now denies.

May you offer to testify? May you testify if you are subpoenaed? May you or must you testify if the court orders you to? If you are the judge, should you order Joe's first lawyer to testify upon the prosecutor's offer of proof?

8.   Joe Mitchell's lawyers received a call yesterday from Donald Weston. Weston is a semi-retired attorney at a major law firm. Weston said that he was consulted by a client last week and felt obliged to share with you the contents of that conversation. (He told you that he doesn't "give a damn" whether what he tells you is within the requirements of the attorney-client privilege or not.) His client is a prominent local psychiatrist who is treating Brooke Thompson. The psychiatrist told

Weston that he was helping Brooke Thompson "work through" her feelings of guilt about her killing her stepdaughter and wanted to know whether he had any legal exposure for failing to come forward with this information in order to save Mitchell. The psychiatrist told him that whether or not he had exposure, he would never reveal what a patient told him, except, of course, within a conversation that was itself privileged, such as his conversation with his attorney. Weston was unable to come forward.

What ethical issues for Mitchell's lawyers are involved in this situation? Must Mitchell's lawyers report Weston under Rule 8.3?

9.   Assume you have settled the *MacIntyre* case for Jesse. For his own reasons, the defendant wants to transfer the settlement check directly into Jesse's bank account, a plan to which you have no objections and which serves Jesse's interests. Jesse previously told you where she banks and her account number.

May you inform the defendant of Jesse's bank and account number?

10.   Easterfield declined to pay a fee of $8,200 for research you did on the criminal penalties for arson in Nita City, claiming that he had not authorized the work. You remember that he did authorize the work.

Two of Easterfield's properties have burned down in last year, allowing him to collect $230,000 in insurance.

May you sue Easterfield and reveal, either in your pleadings or in your testimony, that Easterfield was interested in the criminal penalties for arson?

11.   Assume that Easterfield told you credibly that he wanted the research done because a good friend was facing arson charges in another part of the state. Easterfield then engaged in an arson plot that ruined one of the partnerships he participated in. Another partner sues *you*, as well as Easterfield, on a number of theories.

May you reveal what Easterfield told you in the case brought by this third party?

12.   Jesse tells you that she really needs a cigarette, has no money, and that she knows how to pry a pack out of the machine in the lobby of the diner across the street from your office. You tell her that she's crazy, but she just smiles and tells you to wait a minute and she'll be right back. May you report her intention to the store owner?

Must you, under any the provisions of any American jurisdiction?

13.   Six months after you filed suit for Jesse MacIntyre, she tells you in anger that she made the whole thing up, that she can't stand you any more and wants you to withdraw, and that she knows a lawyer named Pierce (whom you believe to have ethics of a scorpion) who can continue the case in the manner she prefers.

What are your obligations?

14.   You have negotiated a deal for Easterfield for a line of credit secured by mortgages on a number of properties, which the bank had appraised by a respected local appraiser. After the deal was complete, but before Easterfield had drawn down the entire line of credit, he tells you that he "got to" the appraiser who, for a "reasonable consideration," vastly over-appraised the property. You are sure you mentioned the appraised value of the property during the negotiations.

       What are your obligations? Would they be any different if it was the appraiser who admitted the payoff to you?

15.   The plaintiffs are about to take Marlow's deposition in the *MacIntyre* case. She is quite favorably disposed to Easterfield and comes to your office the day before the deposition to be "prepared" for the deposition.

       May you report to Easterfield what occurs during the preparation session? May the plaintiff's attorneys inquire into the contents of your preparation session with Marlow?

16.   Assume that Jesse was suing the club for employment discrimination. The club is a Nita corporation. You represent the club. The plaintiff notices Marlow's deposition.

       What issues surround your preparation of Marlow to testify?

17.   Recall the interview with Easterfield concerning the development of Bloomsbury Gardens. In the course of the interview, Easterfield told you that he intended to falsify an environmental impact statement in order to get approval for the project. He said that the "umbrella" under which he was developing the complex, was a privately held corporation of which he was president, director, and held a large minority interest. At the end of the interview, he told you that he intended to proceed with the false statement.

       What issues of confidentiality are implicated in this situation?

PROBLEM SET J.
CONFLICT OF INTEREST: CIVIL

1.   You are a member of a large law firm. Jesse MacIntyre is referred to you by Reverend Taylor. She tells you about her encounter with Easterfield. She wants to file a claim against him for unlawful discharge. Reverend Taylor, who accompanies Jesse to your office, says that contributions from his parish will fund the most aggressive litigation that you can mount. You do a conflicts check on Easterfield. Your firm has offices in several states. You discover that in one state in which your firm has an office, your firm represents a real estate investment trust in which Mr. Easterfield is an officer, a major shareholder, and a member of the board of directors. You take this fact to your managing partner. The managing partner says that the firm would very much like to obtain the Archdiocese as a client. If the firm does well on this case, the Bishop may bring the Archdiocese's legal problems to the firm. Your senior partner tells you to "work it out" so that the firm can represent Jesse and continue to represent the corporation in Florida, with which Easterfield is associated.
        What should you do?

2.   Easterfield comes to your law firm to tell you that he may have a problem. Last weekend, he fired a household employee, Jesse MacIntyre. He is worried that Ms. MacIntyre may sue him. Easterfield tells you that a Reverend Taylor is encouraging her to sue. Easterfield says that he wants to litigate this case to the hilt.
        Your firm has managed to obtain the Archdiocese as a client. You very much want to keep that business. You also want to keep Mr. Easterfield as a client. You decide to do whatever you can to keep both clients. The associates who interviewed Easterfield are worried about a potential conflict.
        As senior ethics counsel to the firm, advise the associates who interviewed Easterfield.

3.   You have agreed to represent Mr. Easterfield in the scenario described in Problem 2 above. Mr. Easterfield has been advised of your representation of the Archdiocese and has waived the possible conflict. You did not think that it was necessary to obtain the consent of the Archdiocese because it was not involved in this case. When the Archdiocese hears of your decision to represent Mr. Easterfield, you receive a call from the bishop. The bishop asks you how you could have agreed to represent Mr. Easterfield against a poor soul like Jesse MacIntyre who is struggling to better herself. He threatens to move the Archdiocese's business to the firm that has agreed to represent Jesse. Ethics counsel for your firm advises you to withdraw from the representation of Easterfield in order to preserve the steady stream of business that will be provided by the bishop. Ethics counsel tells you, "If we have to make a choice, we'll go with the client who provides us with the most financial support."
        What should you say to the firm's ethics counsel?

Exercises & Problems in Professional Responsibility

PROBLEM SET K.
ADVERTISING AND SOLICITATION

1.   When Jesse MacIntyre got into the cab to go to see Reverend Taylor after leaving the Easterfields', she picked up a newspaper that was lying on the back seat. Although she was still extremely upset, she began to read the newspaper. Paging through the paper, she came upon the following advertisement:

NEED A LAWYER TO STAND UP TO YOUR BOSS?
THE EMPLOYEE'S LAW FIRM WILL GET JUSTICE FOR YOU

"Let the Employee's Law Firm handle your case. We specialize in suing employers who take advantage of their employees. If you have been fired, you probably have a claim for breach of contract or a claim for employment discrimination against your boss. You may be entitled to back wages and to damages. The Employee's Law Firm will take your case for nothing—only a percentage of what we recover for you. The Employee's Law Firm wins 85 percent of its cases. That's one heck of a batting average. Stand up for your rights. Go with the winners. Call 555-1212 for more information. Certified by the National Association of Employee Advocates."

Jesse tore the ad out of the paper and took it into the Rectory. There she showed it to Reverend Taylor. Reverend Taylor told Jesse that it was too early to discuss a lawsuit. He told Jesse to get some rest at the St. James Home, and that they would talk about what steps to take the next morning.

Have the lawyers of Employee's Law Firm violated their ethical obligations?

2.   Jesse took Reverend Taylor's advice. She went straight to her room at the St. James Home and tried to sleep. But she was unable to sleep because she was so upset. At about 2 A.M., she decided to turn on the television in her room. Coincidentally, the first thing that she saw on the television was an ad for the Employee's Law Firm.

In the commercial, a man who identified himself as Lee Jones, a prominent attorney from Boston, spoke to the camera:

Hi, I'm Lee Jones. I try cases all over the country. I've helped a lot of people get their jobs back. When I come to Nita City, I always make a point of going to see my friends at the Employee's Law Firm. I get a lot of pointers from them about how to make bosses do right by their employees. If I had a case in Nita City, and I couldn't afford to hire Lee Jones, I'd hire the Employee's Law Firm. You can count on them. The lawyer will take you, and a person of your choice, to dinner so that you may discuss your case with the firm's lawyer in a relaxed home. This should tell you that the Employee's Law Firm cares about you. Call right away. There will be no obligation to accept the offer of the firm's services. Call 555–1212 right now. Operators are on duty.

Any ethical problems?

3.   After seeing the commercial, Jesse picked up the phone and called the Employee's Law Firm's number. The phone was answered by Tina Jones, who identified herself as "the lawyer on duty." The following conversation took place between Jesse and Ms. Jones:

Jesse: I've got a problem. I've been fired.

Jones: That's too bad. Who fired you?

Jesse: Mr. Easterfield.

Jones: Is that "Old Moneybags" Easterfield?

Jesse: Yes.

Jones: You may have a good case. Can we meet tomorrow? How about an early breakfast? By the way, what's your name and where do you live?

Jesse: My name is Jesse MacIntyre. I'm living now at the St. James Home. I'm not sure that I can meet you for breakfast. I'd like to talk to Reverend Taylor about this.

Jones: You can talk to him later. Let's not get the church involved. Let's meet tomorrow morning.

Jesse: O.K. I guess that it will be all right.

Jones: 8 A.M. at the West Egg—Nita.

Ethical problems?

4.   After this conversation, Jesse felt better. She went to sleep. She got up early the next morning. As she was walking through the lobby of the home on her way to the West Egg, Sister Mary, a member of the home's staff, handed her an envelope. The envelope was addressed to Jesse and was from Tina Jones. It read:

"I just wanted to remind you about our meeting today at 8 A.M. Our firm is very interested in your case. As you know, our firm specializes in employment lawsuits. We will do a wonderful job for you. You won't be sorry if you hire us to represent you."

Permissible?

5.   When Jesse arrived at the West Egg, the events of the day before overwhelmed her. She began to cry. She heard someone say, "You must be Jesse." She turned and saw a woman dressed in a black suit, pink shirt, flowered scarf, dark glasses, and pointed shoes. She identified herself as Tina Jones.

Jones gave Jesse her handkerchief. They sat down and ordered breakfast. Jones asked Jesse what happened. Jesse told her. Jones then said, "I'd like to take your case. You don't have to pay anything up front. We get paid a percentage of what we recover for you—the standard 40 percent. I brought along a retainer agreement. You'll have to sign it if you want me to represent you. It'll protect both of us. By the way, you don't have to worry, I'm the best and our firm wins cases against big shots all the time." Jesse said, "Maybe I should talk to Reverend Taylor." Jones replied, "Come on, what does the clergy know about lawyers?" Jesse then signed the retainer agreement.

Jesse returned to the St. James Home. She met Reverend Taylor in the hallway and told him that she had retained Ms. Jones and the Employee's Law Firm. Reverend Taylor was shocked. He said, "I thought ambulance chasing was illegal. I'm calling the disciplinary authorities. I want you to talk to our lawyer, Ms. Demetral."

How are the Employee's Law Firm and Ms. Jones likely to do before the disciplinary committee?

6.   Assume that Jesse was unable to find a lawyer to represent her. Because the statute of limitation was fast approaching, she decided to file a pro se wrongful discharge case against Mr. Easterfield.

The Employees Law Firm retains a paralegal to review all complaints filed in the Nita City Circuit Court. The purpose of this review is to find cases in which plaintiffs who might be entitled to substantial damages do not have counsel. Shortly after Jesse filed her complaint, the Employees Law Firm's investigator, Joe Shades, saw it at the Nita City Clerk's office. Seeing that Easterfield was the defendant, Shades contacted the law firm lead counsel, Sam Brown. Shades and Brown went immediately to see Jesse. At the meeting Brown told Jesse that he wanted to handle her case because he did not like the way that Easterfield treated his employees. Brown offered to take the case for one-half of his usual fee. After the meeting, Jesse agreed to retain the Employees Law Firm. Easterfield's lawyer hears how Jesse came to retain the Employee's Law Firm. He asks his lawyers to file a disciplinary complaint against the Employees Law Firm. Will the disciplinary complaint be sustained?

Exercises & Problems in Professional Responsibility

PROBLEM SET L.
SPEAKING TO THE PRESS

1. Joe Mitchell has learned that the state's attorney of Nita County is investigating him for his wife's shooting. He asked his attorney, Chris Freeman, how he should respond to the investigation. In addition to telling Joe that he should not speak to the police, Freeman suggests a "public relations strategy" much like that employed in recent high-profile cases. He suggests hiring a public relations firm to help generate favorable publicity about Joe and unfavorable publicity about the state's attorney of Nita City. The public relations firm of Bird and Grey is retained. Bird and Grey advise holding a press conference at which Freeman will read the following statement

> It has come to my attention that a false accusation of murder may soon be brought against my client, Joe Mitchell. This false accusation will be made because the Nita County state's attorney's is seeking the easy way out. Instead of thoroughly investigating this case, the State's Attorney will prosecute the most likely, but most innocent, suspect.

2. Immediately after the indictment of Joe Mitchell for the murder of Leslie Thompson, Mitchell, the State's Attorney of Nita County held a news conference to announce the indictment. During this news conference, the state's attorney said the following:

> I would like to respond to the public comments made just a few days ago by Mr. Freeman, Joe Mitchell's lawyer. Today we announce the indictment of Joe Mitchell for the brutal and senseless shooting of Leslie Thompson Mitchell, the daughter of the late Judge Thompson. You will recall that this crime shocked our peaceful and law-abiding community. This indictment is based upon the testimony of Brooke Thompson, Leslie's stepmother, who witnessed the crime and who identified Joe Mitchell as the murderer. Joe Mitchell, as some of you know, is an itinerant writer who was living in one of our city's rooming houses for transients at the time the crime was committed. Mr. Mitchell, as one might expect, has denied involvement in the crime. He has refused to cooperate with our investigation, even declining to give the police a complete account of his whereabouts at the time of the murder. The public can expect vigorous prosecution of Mr. Mitchell. I will see to it that justice is done and that our streets remain safe for the decent and law-abiding citizens of Nita City.

3. Immediately after hearing the prosecutor speak at the news conference, Joe Mitchell's attorney called a press conference at which he said the following:

> Today, the state's attorney of Nita County held a press conference at which he announced the indictment of my client and during which he described the allegations against my client. My client is not guilty. At trial, we will show that Brooke Thompson is a liar and that her testimony is motivated by a long-standing hatred for Joe. In fact, there is good reason to believe that Brooke Thompson herself committed the crime. We also have reason to believe that

the state may seek to turn a convicted felon, John Bierman, against Joe Mitchell. This would be but another example of the prosecution's reprehensible use of "jailhouse snitch testimony." Under our system of justice, you are innocent unless proven guilty beyond a reasonable doubt. Joe Mitchell is innocent. He will prevail at trial unless the state's attorney is able, prior to trial, to poison the minds of the citizens of Nita County.

After hearing about these press conferences, the Nita disciplinary authorities brought charges against the prosecutor and against defense counsel for violating professional rules of conduct regarding pretrial publicity.

What is the likely result?

PROBLEM SET M.
THE DUTY TO REPORT MISCONDUCT

1.   You are Jesse MacIntyre's second lawyer. She tells you that her first lawyer took a thousand dollars from her and two weeks later told her that he would not represent her. When you call him and ask him what is going on, he tells you that he spent five hours investigating the case, and then decided that it was not worth bringing. He tells you that he told Jesse that the thousand dollars was a non-refundable retainer and that he charged two hundred dollars an hour. Jesse tells you that he said no such thing and tells you to do what you can to get her money back.

      What should you say when you call her first lawyer back? Should you report Jesse's first lawyer to the disciplinary authorities? Must you report Jesse's first lawyer? May you threaten to report him if he does not return the payment?

2.   Jesse MacIntyre tells you that there was more. During a visit to her first lawyer, the lawyer told her that he would do the case for 10 percent of the recovery if she spent some time with him "at the No-Tell motel." She refused. Jesse tells you that she found the whole thing humiliating and does not want you to pursue the matter or mention it to anyone.

      Should you report the matter to the disciplinary authorities? Must you?

3.   You represent Joe Mitchell. It turns out that Officer Slyviak grew up in your neighborhood and that you went to high school together. One day, a month after Joe was arrested, Slyviak tells you that he wants to speak with you and names a downtown bar. There he tells you that he had in fact located Jerry Young and brought him in to speak with the prosecutor. After a perfunctory conversation, the prosecutor told Young to take a bus to Alaska for the duration. Slyviak tells you that if you say that he told you this, he will deny it, Slyviak claims, persuasively, "I'm a whole lot better liar from the stand than you are, buddy. I've had more practice."

      You discuss this conversation with Joe, who tells you that he wants you to try to use this information to "get me a deal." He orders you not to make this conversation public. "I don't want to go toe-to-toe with the prosecutor and the police on this; we'll lose for sure." When you mention reporting it to the disciplinary authorities, he becomes adamant. "Do *not* do that," he tells you. "It will only serve to make the prosecutors bear down harder on me."

      You know that the judge in your case has a reputation for resolving all disputes of fact that pit policemen against others, in favor of the police.

      What should you do? Explain it to Joe.

4.   Again, you represent Joe Mitchell. This time, Joe tells you that before you began to represent him, he was approached by another lawyer, a prominent local attorney named Paulette Grogan. Grogan offered to represent him for free in return for exclusive rights to write Joe's story should he be acquitted. Joe said that was fine with him, but then came to dislike Grogan and fired her. During the time Grogan was representing Joe, Joe and Grogan had both told the police that they didn't want Joe to make any further statements without his lawyer present. Through the use of effective, but marginal pressure tactics, the police extracted a damaging admission in a conversation with Joe of which Grogan was not given notice.

Exercises & Problems in Professional Responsibility

You want Grogan to testify that she was representing Joe at the time the admission was made. You think that there is a good chance that this would lead to the suppression of the admission. You mention to Joe that you have concerns about the ethics of Grogan's contract with him under Rule 1.8(d) and you are considering reporting Grogan to the disciplinary authorities. Joe says, "Are you kidding? We need the testimony. Keep your mouth shut."

Should you report Grogan? Must you report her?

5. You represent Ross Easterfield. Jesse MacIntyre has managed to find herself one of the worst lawyers in town, John Ashley. Easterfield knows this and is happy that your opponent is so notoriously incompetent. You believe that Ashley was under the influence of alcohol during his deposition of Easterfield and therefore, failed to ask many of the most obvious questions. (He learned nothing of Easterfield's brushes with the law, for example, and also never asked Easterfield what exactly he said to the ABC Employment Agency.) You described the whole performance to your partner as "an embarrassment to the profession."

The next day, you were having lunch at the Bar Association restaurant with a friend who is also a lawyer. The subject of Ashley arose. Your friend told that she is currently representing someone who had previously retained Ashley. Your friend tells you that Ashley "stole her blind . . . commingled funds . . . the whole shebang." She tells you that he doesn't believe in "*Himmel*-squealing," but that she had really told Ashley off.

Should you report Ashley? Must you? Must you report your friend?

6. After the *MacIntyre* case is over, Ashley's wife comes to see you about a divorce. She describes enduring three years of gruesome physical abuse at his hands. She has moved out of the house with her infant child.

Assuming that you are competent, may you represent her in the her divorce action? Should you report Ashley to the disciplinary authorities? Must you?

7. You are an associate in the law firm that represents Ross Easterfield. Ross drops by the office of the partner handling his case. He has a contented grin on his face and tells the partner in your presence to expect a serious settlement call soon. Ross closes the door and tells you with a wink that one of his "people" had just had a chat with Jesse's lawyer and that they had worked out a "sweet deal." Under the arrangement, the lawyer would convince Jesse to settle for $50,000, from which the lawyer would receive his 40 percent fee. Two months later, they would send the lawyer a second $20,000 check for his "good offices."

The partner looks nervously at you and says, "Just keep me out of this."

Easterfield says, "All you have to do is sign the settlement papers."

After Easterfield leaves, you tell your partner that you have a sick feeling about this. The partner tells you to "keep a lid on this" since Easterfield is an important client with "unorthodox, but effective" methods. The partner forbids you to interfere or mention this to anyone.

If the instructions stand, what should you do?

PROBLEM SET N.
CONFLICTS OF INTEREST: CRIMINAL

1.   You have agreed to represent both Mitchell and Bierman. Both have signed written waivers of any conflicts which might arise. On the day before trial, the prosecutor approaches you with a deal for Bierman. The prosecutor offers Bierman immunity if he will testify against Joe Mitchell. Despite the fact that you represent both defendants, you feel that you must convey the offer to Bierman. In response to the offer Bierman says, "I'd like a few days to think about it. What do you think? Don't tell Joe about this."
       How should you respond to Bierman's reaction to the state's offer of immunity?

2.   You meet with Mitchell and Bierman to prepare them for trial. You have decided, with your clients, that both of them will testify at trial. Out of the blue, Joe asks whether it will be in his best interest for Bierman to testify. Joe is concerned about the jury hearing about Bierman's record and knowing that he (Joe) was spending time with a convicted felon.
       How should you respond to Joe's concern about whether Bierman should testify?

3.   During trial, the eyewitness testimony against Bierman is much weaker than that against Joe, probably due to the fact that Brooke knew Joe and did not know Bierman.
       How should you conduct your cross-examination of the eyewitness? May you highlight the differences between the witness' testimony: *Mitchell v. Bierman*? May you downplay those differences? How should you argue the reliability of the eyewitness testimony during the closing argument?

4.   Prior to trial, the judge asks you "as an officer of the court" whether you can foresee any potential conflicts that might prevent you from providing effective assistance of counsel to both defendants.
       How should you respond?

PROBLEM SET O.
JUDICIAL ETHICS

1.   *People v. Mitchell* is assigned to Judge Green. Judge Green was a colleague and friend of the late Judge Thompson, Leslie's father and Brooke's husband.

   A.   Assume that Mitchell's lawyer has moved for the disqualification of Judge Green. Should the motion be granted? Are any additional facts necessary to decide the motion?

   B.   Assume that there has been no motion to disqualify. Instead, at the first hearing in the case, Judge Green announced her past association with Judge Thompson and asked the attorneys if they had any objection to her involvement in the case. Both prosecution and defense counsel stated on the record and in open court, that they were satisfied with Judge Green's impartiality.
   Can Judge Green hear the case?

   C.   Now assume that Judge Green is not an old friend of Judge Thompson. Instead, Judge Green is a former county prosecutor, appointed to the bench only two months prior to the *Mitchell* indictment. Joe's attorney asks Judge Green to disqualify herself, on the ground that she served in the prosecutor's office along with the same lawyers who are now handling the *Mitchell* case.
   Should the judge grant the motion? Would it make any difference if Judge Green had been appointed after Mitchell's indictment?

   D.   Judge Green lives on Madison Street, about a mile from the Thompson residence. Assume that the judge did not know any of the Thompsons and was unaware that the shooting had occurred.
   May Judge Green sit? Would it make a difference if Judge Green had read newspaper accounts of the shooting the day after it occurred?

2.   *MacIntyre v. Easterfield* is assigned to Judge Brown. Judge Brown was a successful trial attorney and a partner in a prominent law firm before taking the bench ten years ago.

   A.   Assume that Judge Brown was a partner in the law firm now representing Jesse MacIntyre. The lawyer representing Jesse came to the firm three years ago.
   May Judge Brown continue to preside over the case? What if the lawyer representing Jesse came to the firm twenty years ago and practiced regularly with Judge Brown?

   B.   Now assume that Judge Brown is a member of the Nita City Athletic Club, and has occasionally had lunch with Ross Easterfield.
   May Judge Brown sit? What if Judge Brown had been on the committee of the club that hired Lee Marlow?

   C.   Now assume that Judge Brown is on the board of directors of the St. James Home for Women.
   May Judge Brown sit on the *MacIntyre* case?

Exercises & Problems in Professional Responsibility

D.   Judge Brown is a wealthy individual with many investments and financial interests. Among Judge Brown's holdings is a limited partnership share in a luxury condominium development in Nita City. Ross Easterfield is also a limited partner, and this fact is known to Judge Brown.

May Judge Brown sit in *MacIntyre v. Easterfield*? What if Ross were the general partner? What other factors might influence the outcome of a motion to disqualify?

E.   Assume that Judge Brown is the judge who took Jesse MacIntyre's guilty plea in the armed robbery case.

May Judge Brown sit in *MacIntyre v. Easterfield?* What if Judge Brown had been the prosecutor in that case?

3.   Brooke Thompson is evicting a tenant from one of her apartment buildings. When the case is called in eviction court, the judge says, "Are you any relation to the late Judge Thompson?" When Brooke answers affirmatively, the judge replies, "I have some old photographs of your late husband. Why don't you come see them in my chambers when this case is over." After the eviction hearing, Brooke does come to chambers to look at the old photographs. She and the judge do not discuss the eviction case.

Has there been any misconduct?

4.   Is it proper for Judge Brown to sit on the board of directors of the St. James Home? On the board of the Nita City Athletic Club? What restrictions are there on Judge Brown's participation? How would those restrictions apply if Judge Brown were on the board of the Nita Judge's Association?

5.   Judge Brown, prior to taking the bench, was an outspoken advocate of women's rights, and was active in the Nita Abortion Rights Association.

A.   May Judge Brown continue her membership in the Nita Abortion Rights Association? May Judge Brown serve on the board of directors of the Nita Family Planning Clinic, which is frequently the target of anti-abortion protestors?

B.   After taking the bench, Judge Brown wrote a law review article on abortion rights, stating in part:

> *Roe v. Wade* was a terrible decision, and it has ultimately damaged the cause of women's rights. The question of abortion rights should have been left up to state legislatures. I believe unequivocally in the right to choice, but that right would be better protected through democratic means, as opposed to through undemocratic federal courts.

Has Judge Brown done anything improper? What if the above paragraph had appeared in a letter to the editor of a local newspaper?

C.   Judge Brown has been nominated to the federal district court. At her confirmation hearing, she is asked about her views on abortion.

Can she answer? Can she direct the senators to her writings on the subject? Can she repeat the above paragraph?

D. Judge Brown is extremely telegenic and has been asked to serve as a "trial commentator" for a cable television network. Judge Brown agrees, but says that she will only comment on cases outside Nita. She will be paid a fee.

6.   Judges are elected in the State of Nita.

A.   Ross Easterfield was prosecuted for criminal housing fraud in YR-11. Ross pled guilty to a reduced charge, and was given probation. It was later discovered that Ross had been a significant contributor to the Judge's reelection campaign, but this fact was not disclosed to the prosecutor.

Has there been any impropriety?

B.   Judge Green is running for reelection. One of her authorized campaign leaflets states: "Domestic abuse will not end unless we keep qualified women on the bench. Vote for Judge Green."

Is the leaflet proper? What if the leaflet said: "Judge Green has never given probation in a domestic abuse case"? What if it said: "Judge Green will not give probation in any domestic abuse cases"?

C.   Judge Brown is not up for reelection, but Judge Green is. Judge Brown believes that Judge Green has been unfairly targeted by misogynist organizations.

May Judge Brown speak out on behalf of Judge Green? May Judge Brown ask practicing lawyers to do so? May Judge Green recruit her own campaign surrogates?

7.   A.   Judge Brown owns 1,000 shares of stock in the Nita City National Bank. She always excuses herself from cases involving the bank.

Any problems?

B.   The State of Nita has the lowest judicial salaries in the United States. Judge Green is an outstanding dog trainer and has produced many champion dogs.

May she supplement her income by selling her dogs for a profit? May she incorporate her breeding business? May she give dog training classes, for a fee, at the local community center?

C.   Judge Brown's husband is an investor in a number of enterprises, including a distillery, a sports bar, an insurance company, a riverboat casino, and a "topless" nightclub. Judge Brown knows that she cannot sit in any cases involving companies in which her husband holds an interest.

Any problems? Is there a distinction between publicly and closely held companies?

D.   The State of Nita requires all of its judges to file annual financial disclosure statements, including all financial holdings of the judge, the judge's spouse, and minor children residing in the judge's home. Judge Brown's husband refuses to cooperate, and will not provide the requested financial information.

What should Judge Brown do?